THE 2e REP

FRENCH FOREIGN LEGION PARATROOPERS

By Yves DEBAY
translated from the French by Alan McKay

HISTOIRE & COLLECTIONS

CONTENTS

The Légionnaires Parachutistes are modest people in spite of their brilliant service record. They are hard workers and are faithful to the old adage that 'toil saves blood'; they are always ready for the tasks that the Republic entrusts to them. When this is the case, the mission is carried out with the true efficiency of the old Legion. They are modest and proud of the work they do! This pride in their service and success is encouraged within the regiment so that the old and the new legionaries are steeped in it.

This is what gives the REP its strength.

Often they would prefer the media and the cameras forget them so that they can get on with the work in hand more calmly… but it is difficult to avoid your own legend.

Nowadays, and far too often in their opinion, the Green Berets of the 2e Régiment Etranger de Parachutistes find themselves in the limelight and in this modern world of ours the result is not always a happy one.

The myth of the superman without moods or of military romanticism does not go away easily, and even if it is to be found in some of the legionaries, the 2e REP is first and foremost an exceptional fighting unit in the service of France.

The aim of this book is to present the 2e REP just as it is, without adding to the mystique. I hope I have succeeded. War is not waged with choirboys, but it is in this warrior and specialist community that I found the values which have often disappeared from our society: simplicity, disinterestedness, efficiency and above all the enormous human warmth of men shaped by ordeal.

Yves Debay

Supple, feline and manoeuvring are the qualities which the French parachutists like to give themselves. It is true that the attitude of this Legion parachutist, watching the movements of US Marines during the PHYBLEX 87 exercise in the distance, has everything of the big cat. The man belongs to the 4th Company and is holding a FR-F1. His position is that of an observer not a marksman.
(Yves Debay)

INDOCHINA

A platoon of the 2e BEP crossing a 'rach' during *Operation Rouleaux* (Rollers) in August 1950. The legionaries very quickly got to like this countryside, more than any other, where so many left their lives.
(© ECPAD/France)

At the end of WWII, the Foreign Legion was a famous and versatile Corps de Troupe, which no longer had to make a reputation. The war which had just finished had also added some laurel leaves to its crown. From Narvik to Bir Hakeim, and from the Levant to the Vosges, the legionary had shown that he was still a shock infantryman *"par excellence"*. However, a new type of soldier had covered himself with glory during the conflict, the paratrooper, overrunning the enemy by dropping from the sky.

The old Legion did not have any paratroopers, whereas there was a pressing need for soldiers with this qualification in Indochina.

Despite the argument of the General Staff, who opposed the rigour and the heaviness of the Legion to the versatility of the paratroopers, the 3e REI set up a parachute company in 1949, under the command of Lieutenant Morin. The die was cast and this new type of soldier entered the legend.: the Legion Parachutist.

At almost the same period, the BEP (*Batallion Etranger de Parachutistes*) was created at Khamisis in Algeria, on 1 July 1948, under the command of Captain Segrétain.

The 2e BEP was created on 1st October 1948 at Sétif. A 3e BEP was set up in April 1949 at Mascara and installed itself shortly afterwards at Sétif where it became the dépôt for the Legion Parachutists committed in the Far East.

It was the time of the French Army without means. The paratroopers jumped from US Army surplus Dakotas and Junkers 52s which had survived the war. A lot of these Legion Parachutists were former together with men from all over Europe.

Many fell for France in Indochina.

Right:
As soon as they arrived
the Paras learned to respect
the Viets. Contrary to what one might
expect, the War in Indochina was not
a colonial war but the beginning
of an ideological one as this shot
taken during *Operation
Rouleaux* shows.
(© ECPAD/France)

3ᵉ REI insigna

Below:
Legionaries from 2ᵉ BEP
moving through the humidity
of the jungle. At any moment
death could strike from
this inextricable greenery.
Note the uniform from
the beginning of the war
with the soft jungle hat
and the US M1 rifle.
(© ECPAD/France)

INDOCHINA

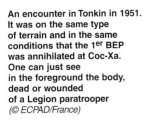

It was in Indochina at the cost of many lives that the epic of the Legion paratroopers was started. As soon as it arrived in Haiphong in November 1948, the 1er BEP was committed to the fighting. For two years the battalion carried out a series of OAP *(Opération aéroportée/Airborne Operations)* getting results which spoke for themselves. Two years after its creation, the 1er BEP entered history in the most tragic fashion.

On 18 September 195, the legionaries jumped over That-Khé, during the operation to evacuate Cao-Bang and along the RC-4 *(Route coloniale/Colonial road)* positions.

It was the moment of sacrifice. Between Dong-Khé and Coc-Xa, the 1er BEP was annihilated in the jungle and the chalk hills. Its honour was safe but the Legionaries were not able to both fight against the superior numbers of Viets and the

incompetence of their command. On 5 October, on Hill 533, a platoon sacrificed itself to enable the unit to retreat. The BEP fell back on the Coc-Xa basin and tried to force its way through a day later across very chaotic terrain. Although suffering terribly they carried out their wounded; they had to climb the chalk cliffs by night… but at odds of one against ten, and the Viets were everywhere. Cut off from each other, without outside support, the sections were annihilated one by one during furious hand to hand fighting. Segretain, the battalion commander was killed as were all the unit commanders. Captain Jeanpierre brought out twenty eight survivors…

The young Legion Parachutists had entered the roll of Honour of the Old Legion by the front door. The 1er BEP was re-created on 1 March 1951 at Hanoi and included an Indochinese company according to the wishes of General de Lattre.

An encounter in Tonkin in 1951. It was on the same type of terrain and in the same conditions that the 1er BEP was annihilated at Coc-Xa. One can just see in the foreground the body, dead or wounded of a Legion paratrooper *(© ECPAD/France)*

INDOCHINA

From left to right:

1er BEP insigna.

2e BEP insigna.

1er CEPML insigna.

The 2e BEP landed at Saigon on 9 February 1949 and was committed into Cambodia and Central Annam where it won its first laurels.

Under the command of Squadron Commander Raffali, the battalion jumped over Gia-Hoi and was violently attacked on the RC-6 at Nghia-Lo. It was on this same road that the two BEPs distinguished themselves during the Hoa-Binh operations.

In January, the 1er BEP fought hand to hand on the Black river. During a cleaning-up operation, to the south of Hanoi, having accepted to lead the 2e

BEP into combat, Major Raffali was mortally wounded and died in Hanoi hospital on 10 September. In 1953, the two BEPs were engaged in Thai country where they managed to gather in the units which were disengaging in the region.

These operations led to the setting-up of the fortified camp at Na-Sam where the Viet-Minh took a hiding. Kept in the general reserve, the two BEPs were nevertheless engaged in combing operations in the Delta.

A line of legionaries moving on during Operation *Tulip* near Cho-Ben in 1951... de Lattre's year where all hopes were allowed. In the delta the heat was overwhelming and a lot of legionaries were victim of the '*coup de bambou*' (Sun Stroke).
(© ECPAD/France)

Above left:
A company headquarters
has been set up on the roof
of this hut during
Operation *Brochet*.
Note the uniform called
'sausage skins',
of British origin.
The expeditionary corps
in Indochina was poor
and had to make do
with what was available.
(© ECPAD/France)

Above right and below:
Unlike the zero-casualties
of our end-of-century wars
totally sterilised
by the media
and the authorities,
the war in Indochina
was covered without
false modesty
by photographers
who like Schoendorfer,
shared the risks.
They have left us poignant
pictorial accounts
showing the degree
of selflessness of these
combatants who
were forgotten
by the Metropole
(© ECPAD/France)

Above:
It was against weapons like this recoilless 57 mm canon,
set up by the 2e BEP during Operation *Dromadaire*,
that Giap was faced with during the siege of Na-Sam.
He quickly learnt his lesson.
(© ECPAD/France)

DIEN-BIEN-PHU
RIGHT TO THE END!

On 21 November 1953, Operation Castor took place. The 1er BEP and the Compagnie Etrangère de Mortier Lourd *(CEPML - the Foreign Legion Heavy Mortar Company)* jumped near a village called Dien-Bien-Phu which had not yet entered history. The 1erBEP was the fer-de-lance of the fortified camp and took part in all the sallies, particularly Operation Pollux.

On 13 March 1954, the Viets attacked in force and surprised head-quarters with its fire-power. The support point at Gabrielle was held by the veterans of the 13e DBLE *(Demi-brigade de la Légion Etrangère/Foreign Legion half brigade)* fell in one night. By trying to counter-attack the 1er BEP lost half its strength. The situation was scarcely better with the CEPML which lost three mortars in three days. The Twilight of the Gods had begun. The units exhausted telmselves with futile counter-attacks which did not stop them from holding their ground desperately despite the Viets' heavy shelling. On Eliane 2, a company held for five days against a whole regiment. On 10 April, the 2e BEP jumped into the furnace. During a counter-attack on Huguette 6, the battalion was wiped out. On 24 April, the remainder of the two BEPs regrouped in the BMEP *(Batallion de Marche Etranger de Parachutistes)* and celebrated Camerone before the final assault.

In the night of 5-6 May, the Legion paratroopers fought their gallant last stand. At 17.00 on 7 May 1954, all was finished; Dien-Bien-Phu had fallen. Leonidas's old saying could just as well apply to this field of blood and mud which had witnessed the end of a world: *'Go and tell Sparta that we fell according to the rules'.*

1976 legionaries fell for France in Indochina. At the end of the conflict the two BEPs were re-created thanks to the influx of volunteers and by the dissolution of the 3e BEP which had arrived in Indochina in June 1954.

On the last 14th July celebrations in Indochina, the 2e BEP received the red fourragère of the Legion d'Honneur before embarking. A page had been turned, but the legionaries had paid with their blood for the right to be numbered in the Pantheon of Elite warriors.

The shots taken at Dien-Bien-Phu speak for themselves.
Remember that the majority of these men did not return
from the Viet prisoner of war camps.
(all photos (© ECPAD/France)

ALGERIA

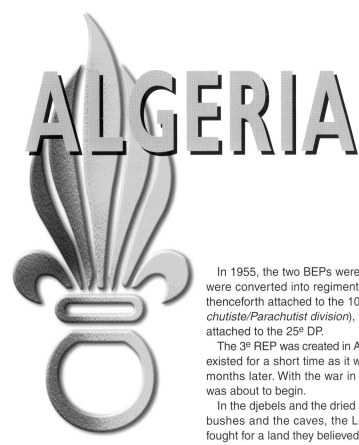

In 1955, the two BEPs were sent to Algeria and were converted into regiments. The 1er REP was thenceforth attached to the 10e DP (*division parachutiste/Parachutist division*), whereas the 2e was attached to the 25e DP.

The 3e REP was created in August 1955 and only existed for a short time as it was disbanded three months later. With the war in Algeria, a new epic was about to begin.

In the djebels and the dried out wadis, the scrub bushes and the caves, the Legion paratroopers fought for a land they believed was French.

Moreover, Algeria was sacred as it was the home of the Legion's Alma mater which had been set up at Sidi Bel Abes. From the first months of 1956, the 1er REP trudged around the Constantine area before going into the Oran and Ouarensis sectors. The

2e REP operated in the Batna and Mac-Mahon sectors near Philippeville, where it lost its first legionary.

The Legion parachutists adapted quickly to this new type of war where information was of the essence. Where the conscript units quartered the terrain and tried to win the war of hearts, parachutists, legionaries, marine and air commandos made up the intervention units which made life hard for the Katiba infiltrating their way from Morocco and Tunisia. Even if they were not up to the Viets, the rebels were well-armed by the eastern block and fought courageously.

The MG-42s supplied by the Czechs or Tito's Yugoslavia killed more than one French green beret; but the legionaries nearly always had the upper hand even if they had to look for the fellaghas in the darkest caves.

Previous page:
**Trudging around the djebel.
When they returned
from Indochina,
the Legion paratroopers
very quickly learnt
to combat
this new adversary
in an environment
of scorched scrub and rocks.
They took over rapidly.**
(© ECPAD/France)

Right:
**Guelma, 1958,
the victor and the loser.
This 'fell' is happy
to have escaped death.
He is carrying the weapons
of his less fortunate comrades.
The legionary from
the 1er REP has taken over
an MG 34 machine gun.**
(© ECPAD/France)

Below:
**FM 24/29 set up in typical
Algerian countryside.
At the time the carrier
was a young legionary.**
(© ECPAD/France)

ALGERIA

In 1957, the FLN tried to set itself up in Algiers using its usual method: terror. The authorities were overwhelmed and entrusted the delicate task of fighting against terrorism to the Paras especially the 1er REP.

Under the command of Colonel Jeanpierre, the Green Berets fought an unconventional war where the surviving veterans of Indochina worked marvels using the Viet-Minh's methods.

From 14 January 1957, the legionaries quartered the Casbah and patrolled the popular quarters of Belcourt, la Redoute, Isly and Agha. Check-points, searches and identity controls were the daily tasks during that period. During the night the REP exploited its information. *"Great thinkers"* have criticised the methods which were some-times used by the units engaged in this difficult fight, but a lot of legionaries had seen the torn bodies of children killed by the terrorists' bombs or the horribly mutilated bodies of Algerians tortured by the FLN. The REP therefore carried out its mission with efficiency and without any qualms. In a few months the results were satisfactory and the Algerois were reassured.

Just time to take part in the 14th July parade and a bit of clearing up in the Ain-Taya region before coming back to Algiers. After breaking the general strike and decapitating the terrorist general staff, the Legion parachutists captured Yusuf Saadi and Ali la Pointe, the last rebel chiefs. Algiers had been pacified, the 1er REP returned to the djebel with relief.

Previous page top left:
The Parachutists preferred trudging around the Jebel to doing police work... Nevertheless, the 1er REP was twice engaged in Algiers alongside the 10e DP.
(2e REP archives)

Previous page bottom:
'Leopards' in the Casbah. At first the population was hesitant, but soon accepted the presence of the parachutists in the quarter.
(2e REP archives)

Right:
Photographs of the legionaries wearing white képis operating in Algeria are relatively rare. Here the soldiers of the REP help soldiers from an infantry regiment carry out a routine check.
(2e REP archives)

Below:
By their continual presence, the Legion paratroopers reassured the population and prevented the FLN from setting off a widespread general strike leading to an insurrection.
(2e REP archives)

SUEZ

Top:
**Legionaries boarding
the *Jean-Bart*. The weapons
and the equipment are typical
of the period. MAS-49 rifle
and MAT 49 machine pistol.**
(Képi Blanc)

Below:
**Against a background
of burning refineries set alight
by the Air Force,
LCUs of the 'Royale' loaded
with legionaries head
for the beaches.**
((© ECPAD/France)

During the summer of 1956, the 1er REP was called back from the djebel where it had carried out several helicopter operations, to be regrouped on the Algerian coast. There they trained in amphibious operations with the help of Navy landing barges and Buffalo landing craft which had survived the Pacific.

After a few false alarms, the regiment, under the command of Lieutenant-Colonel Brothier, boarded the battleship Jean-Bart on 31 October 1956. Reservists joined them, including France's youngest deputy who had left the benches of the Assemblée

Nationale for the uncomfortable curves of the battleship.

France and Great Britain had just launched *Operation Musketeer*, whose aim was to recapture the Suez Canal which Nasser had just nationalised. The Chiefs of staffs' aim was also to destabilise the Rais, who had been giving considerable help to the Algerian rebellion.

On 6 November 1956, at dawn, the aeroplanes of the *Royale* (nickname for the French navy) and the Fleet Air Arm bombed Egyptian military installations. While the heavy guns of the *Jean-Bart* were pounding the beaches, barges and landing craft filled with legionaries hurried to the beaches. The objective was the Casino at Port Fuad. At 6 a.m., the legionaries of the 1st Company under Captain Martin landed.

There was scarcely any resistance and the legionaries joined up with other great warriors, the paratroopers of the 2e RPC *(Regiment parachutiste colonial/Colonial Parachutist Regiment)* under the legendary Colonel Château-Jaubert, called *'Colan'*, who had jumped the previous day.

Right:
The first wave of the 1ᵉ REP's assault unit consisted of the 1ˢᵗ company which, here, is landing from a Buffalo.
(Képi Blanc)

Bottom:
'Landing in the Land of the Pharaohs'. Port Fuad was not Omaha Beach and the legionaries moved inland very quickly without meeting any real organised resistance.
(© ECPAD/France)

BEACH LANDING FOR THE REP

19

SUEZ

ON THE CANAL!

A 106 mm recoil-less canon mounted on a Jeep threatening a target on the other side of the Canal.
(Képi Blanc)

Port Fuad was quickly cleared, the Egyptian soldiers very rapidly raising their arms in surrender to the 'little perfume-smelling French soldiers', as Nasser's radio had scoffed.

The REP received the order to head for the south, along the Canal. It reached El Cap, code PK 37, without meeting any great resistance on 7 November where it was surprised by the cease-fire. The Russians were threatening London and Paris with a shower of rockets and Washington had sent its first super carrier to Alexandria, the *USS Forrestal*. Faced with these threats or bluffs, the politicians backed down. Once again the victorious soldiers felt betrayed. From 10 November onwards, the companies of the 1er REP were replaced by UNO observers.

With the exception of Dien-Bien-Phu, the fighting on the Canal was the first conventional warfare operation for the Legion paratroopers. With its legionaries aboard armoured vehicles and committed to an amphibious landing and with a squadron of armour from the 2e REC attached to it, Operation Musketeer heralded the type of versatility which was to characterise the REP in 2000.

Above:
Victorious and smiling, these legionaries have got hold of an Egyptian lorry. Their joy was short-lived since the Anglo-French forces had to pull out after pressure from the 'Big Two'.
(Képi Blanc)

Right:
These exceptional colour shots show Buffaloes and AMX-13s attached to the REP for Operation *Musketeer*. Note the 'lizard'-style uniforms and the radio pennants in the colours of the Foreign Legion. The vehicles here have probably been gathered together prior to re-embarkation.
(Képi Blanc)

Centre:
A 2e REC patrol at Port Fuad. At the time the new AMX-13 was one of the best light tanks in the world.
(Képi Blanc)

ALGERIA

In Algeria, the airborne operations (APs) gave way progressively to helicopter-borne operations. The helicopter was still in its infancy but the high command had very quickly realised the advantages that could be gained from the rotary wing. Paras and legionaries invented the principle of 'aero-mobility' and snaps of men in leopard camouflage jackets jumping from Piasecki 'Flying Bananas' or from tubby Sikorskys are always associated with the war in Algeria.

After the Suez interlude, operations carried on in Algeria. In the Sif djebel, in March 1957, the 2e REP destroyed 193 rebels and captured 150 weapons. There followed a series of operations in the Djidjelli region and the Collo forest before returning in May to Tebessa, its usual operational sector.

After the battle for Algiers, the 1er REP found itself, with some relief back in the 'Bled' ('Outbak') to do some clearing up. It was assigned to the Guelma sector on the Morice line, the famous electrified dam on the frontier with Tunisia. Two Katibas were annihilated on 26 February 1959 after ten hours' fighting. 197 outlaws remained on the battlefield. This feat of arms made General Vanuxem say: The legionaries of the 1er REP, by beating all the figthing records in Algeria, have placed their regiment in the forefront of the French Army's assault troops. On Camerone day, the 1er REP destroyed a band, at Souk Ahras. Two hundred and sixty outlaws were killed and the weapons of a battalion were captured.

The 2e REP was not to be outdone and destroyed several bands. At Djebel Beni-Shibi, dawn on 27 April saw one of the best results of the war: 199 rebels killed.

But fate hit the 1er REP sorely in Spring 1959 while Legion paratroopers were going from success to success.

During an operation on Djebel Taya on 29 May 1958, Lieutenant-Colonel Jeanpierre's helicopter was shot down. 'Soleil' was no longer [1], a legendary figure in the Legion had disappeared.

1. Corps commander's radio sign.

22

Right:
Legion paratroopers spill out of a Piasecki. The man in the foreground is holding his beret in his hand. .a gesture that all airborne troops were to learn.
(*2e REP archives*)

Centre:
Officers from the REP landing from a Sikorsky during an OHP (Opération héliportée - helicopter operation). During a similar operation, Lt-Colonel Jeanpierre was killed aboard an Alouette II command helicopter.
(*2e REP archives*)

Bottom:
Landing by Sikorsky helicopter on a crest. The few paratroopers dropped by the 'windmill' no doubt cut off the enemy's retreat.
(*2e REP archives*)

A classic scene of a zone being sealed off during the Algerian War. Two 1REP sticks have just been landed by Piasecki 'Flying Banana' helicopters; in the background an scout plane can be made out. The Fell have been spotted and can no longer get out of the trap
(*© ECPAD/France*)

ALGERIA

1959-60 saw the end of the FLN's military power. During a long series of military operations, General Challe won the Algerian War militarily. Here a Fellagha chief has just been captured by legionaries.
(© ECPAD/France)

From 1958 to 1959, operations intensified and the series of operations called *'Pierres Précieuses'* (Precious stones) which lasted almost a year literally got the ALN to its knees.

Practically all the units of the general reserve were engaged in Operation Jumelles (Binoculars) which broke the resistance of the last worn-out Katibas.

Militarily, the war in Algeria could be considered as won and the legionaries had contributed greatly to this. 533 of them had been killed in Algeria.

As a peaceful settlement of the conflict was getting slowly nearer, some of the officers of the 1er REP were beginning to have doubts.

They did not want to go back on their word (after Indochina they had promised never to abandon another part of France), nor leave the pro-French population to the mercy of the blind vengeance of the FLN. Presented almost with a 'fait accompli' (This was Algeria winning its independance despite the prmise not to abandon the French Algerians), Major Denoix de St Marc, did not abandon his men. At the result of the events in Algiers, the 1er REP disappeared from the order of battle of the French Army on 30 April 1961.

As it was disbanded, the Legion paratroopers boarded the trucks which would be taking some of them into captivity, singing *'Non, je ne regrette rien'*.

After the cease-fire, the 2e REP rejoined Bou-Sfer not far from Mers-el-Kebir. It was there that the modern paratroop legionary was born, under the auspices of Lieutenant-Colonel Caillaud, who revolutionised the concept of using TAPs *(Troupes aéroportées/Airborne troops)*, in particular by getting the companies to specialise. In December 1963, the 2e REP went to Calvi, its present garrison town.

ALGERIA

In 1961, the 2e REP still shows its traditional image with this legionary on guard at Bou-Sfer, but it can also be that of a commando, looming out of the night like this 1st company legionary. *(Képi Blanc)*

In 1961, the Legion Paratroop family had broken up. The 1er REP which had led so many fights and given so much blood was no more. In the 2e REP, the wounds were gaping. Militarily, the war in Algeria had been won, but not politically. The legionaries knew that they would have to give up their sacred land of Algeria.

Under the command of Lieutenant-Colonel Chenel, the last operations were carried out in the Constantine sector. Their heart was no doubt no longer in their work, but as always the Legion paratroopers gave all they had. As an old legionary, Lieutenant-Colonel Chenel was able to find the right things to say and sought to preserve the regiment's cohesion.

In September 1961, the 2e REP went to its last garrison on African soil, Bou-Sfer within the walls of Mers-el-Kebir where the REP was given the task of protecting the large strategic base.

It was there, in an Algeria given over to itself, that the regiment's transformation began under the command of Lieutenant-Colonel Caillaud, one of the founding fathers of the 2e REP, a hero of the paratroop saga in Indochina. On 29 March 1963, a new era began for the 2e REP.

Lieutenant-Colonel Caillaud was a visionary and he went about profoundly transforming the regiment from a purely parachute infantry unit into a versatile platoon capable of operating in the shortest delay and on all sorts of terrain.

Whilst still holding on to its TAP (Airborne troops) qualification, the REP had to train in order to be able to intervene in any type of situation or for any type of mission. Elite troops have existed from time immemorial, but the 2e REP became a showcase, thanks to its knowledge of the most modern fighting techniques and to the evolution in TAP concepts which its new corps commander had sought.

The new REP is still a parachute unit and airborne training is still important. This series of photos shows a typical jump session at the beginning of the sixties when the 2e REP was still in Africa.

Right:
stick inspection
(Képi Blanc)

Right:
boarding the Noratlas.
(Képi Blanc)

centre:
'Stand up, hook up!'
**Note the typical
(for the period)
Gueno helmet.**
(Képi Blanc)

Below:
**Going out through the door.
Dropping down
and landing,
always a bit rough.**
(Képi Blanc)

CALVI

In December 1963, the 2e REP, head held high but with a heavy heart, left Algeria for ever. Its new garrison town was Calvi, geographically and climatically an ideal place for training and for use as a rear and for foreign operations. A jump school was opened in Calvi in 1963.

The first teams of professional jumpers, the future CRAP *(Commando de recherche et d'action dans la profondeur/Research and in-depth action Commando)* and later the GCP (Groupe de commandos parachutites/Para commando Group) were created.

Lieutenant-Colonel Caillaud revolutionised the way the paratroopers were used and encouraged the setting up of different training areas for the various specialities such as commandos, anti-tank, hand to hand and night fighting, survival, etc. In this context, the combat companies became specialists.

— The 1st Company became the intelligence company with the aim of gathering information and capable of operating within the enemy lines with in-depth patrols of a few men.

— The 2nd Compagnie specialised in mountain work and included a platoon of ski scouts.

— The 3rd Compagnie was transformed into an amphibious unit specialised in water operations and set up its own platoon of reconnaissance divers.

— The 4th Compagnie was directed towards sabotage and destruction, in order to delay the enemy and then specialised also in sharpshooting.

All this instruction was given to the whole of the regiment with courses. In a few years the REP succeeded in transforming itself and becoming an elite unit, very closely fitting the profile of the sort of unit capable of waging a modern war.

As a tool, the REP has been used intensively at the end of this rather eventful turn of the century.

THE 2e REP IN THE SIXTIES

Top:
One of the first abseiling sessions on the citadel at Calvi... soon to become compulsory for a lot of parachutists.
(Képi Blanc)

Right:
At the CEA recoilless guns gave way to SS-10 missiles mounted on Hotchkiss Jeeps. The CEA turned out to be the regiment's strike unit.
(Képi Blanc)

Top left:
**First trips in a helicopter
with one of the first
versions of the Puma.**
(Képi Blanc)

Above left:
**Instinctive shooting training.
The most modern combat
techniques are now
taught at Calvi**
(Képi Blanc)

Top right:
**First jumps over snow
in the Alps for the 2nd company**
(Képi Blanc)

Right:
**The REP which from 1963
had its own jump school
had its own regimental
jump-masters,
after a course at Toulouse.
Here jump-masters
gather up the SAOs
(Sangle Automatique d'Ouverture -
automatic opening harnesses)
in a Noratlas.**
(Képi Blanc)

KOLWEZI

The 2eREP arrived at Calvi at a time when the international situation was deteriorating because of the antagonism between the two superpowers, the USA and the USSR. The Cold War was more than once rather hot for the 2e REP. Brought up by the veterans of Indochina and Algeria, the 2e REP became a modern combat tool which found fame in various foreign theatres of operation, particularly in Africa.

Lenin once said 'We will turn Europe through Africa', and at the end of the sixties, it was precisely what the Soviets and their satellites had set out to do. To the religious and ethnic troubles of post-colonial Africa was added a series of localised conflicts provoked by the expansion of Soviet interests. Mauritania, Western Sahara, Guinea, Rhodesia, Angola, Zaire, Mozambique and Chad were only different forms of the same conflict where, depending on the circumstances, the tribalism of Old Africa and Animism-Islam antagonism cohabited with, or confronted the Marxists trained at Patrice Lumumba University.

With their brothers-in-arms, the Marines, the Colo-

nial Parachutists from the 3e and 8e RPIMa *(Régiment parachutiste d'infanteriede marine/Ex-colonial airborne infantry Regiment, equiv. Marines)*, the Legion Paras fought wherever French interests were threatened.

Technocrats in Paris liked to use the term 'crisis solving tool', but the 2e REP was without doubt more than that. Its interventions in Africa were above all a matter of men, of the technicalities of war, of local knowledge and… of guts.

Operation Bonite, with its spectacular jump over Kolwezi has remained in everybody's memory.

The *'Tigers'* threaten Katanga!

In May 1978, three thousand Katangese rebels coming from Angola, invested the mining town of Kolwezi. Their object was to destabilise the giant Zaire, by dragging its richest province into another secession. Supported by Cuba and East-Germany, the 'Tigers' of the Congo National Liberation Front

Katanga was coveted particularly for its mineral wealth. Here the jeeps from the scout platoon have arrived at the Gécamines plant at Kamoto-Musonoi. These twin mines produced 60% of the world production of cobalt and 15% of that of copper.
(© ECPAD/France)

(FNLC), led by Nathanael M'Bumba, got hold of the town centre and threatened the Europeans whereas scores of Africans were massacred. As usual, the Zaire Army was routed. Only the elite paratroopers of the 311e Batallion TAP were trounced when they landed after their jump, which indicated that the enemy was well-armed.

President Mobutu was a friend of the West and asked France for military help. President Giscard d'Estaing did not hesitate and gave the 11e DP the go-ahead to launch a rescue operation at more than 7 000 kms from France. The 2e REP was given the alert on 17 May and after a Homeric trip reached Kinshasa on 19 May.

Under the command of Colonel Erulin, the unit consisted of four fighting companies of 138 men, the CCS *(Compagnie de commandement et de soutien/Command and Support Company)* and a reconnaissance platoon. Orders and counter-orders were given and only succeeded in increasing the tension. In the humidity of N'djilli airport, the legionaries had to adapt the Zaire T-10 parachute harness to fit French parachute, while the officers desperately searched for maps of the country. The element of surprise was ruined by press declarations. At Kolwezi, this information relayed by East-German transmitters in Angola gave the signal for the massacre. Any further delay would have had incalculable repercussions. At 3.30 on 19 May, Colonel Erulin and Colonel Gras, the commander of the French Military Mission in Zaire, took the decision to bring the operation forward. *We're going to jump!*

Above right:
Lt Erulin directing operations from his Jeep *(Képi Blanc)*

Right:
As soon as the jump is over, the terrain has to be defended and the rebels chased with vehicles which have arrived in the third wave, or lorries taken over from the mining companies.
(© ECPAD/France)

Bottom: **In front of the huge ant-hills which are typical of Katanga, these legionaries are setting up an 81 mm mortar battery; it was one of the most formidable weapons in the African theatre of operations.**
(© ECPAD/France)

KOLWEZI

Above:
At Kolwezi, the snipers who christened the first FR-F1s had a field day, demoralising their African adversaries, totally bemused by these shots coming out of nowhere.
(© ECPAD/France)

Bottom:
A MAT-49 in his hand, this legionary is protecting himself from the heat and the mosquitoes with a camouflage net.
(© ECPAD/France)

The jump took place on 19 May at 15.30. The first wave - 1re, 2e, 3e Companies, a skeleton Command post and a team from the 13e RDP (Régiment de dragons parachutistes) jumped exactly where they were not expected… on the old aero-club to the north of the town.

The first wave regrouped in record time, at most 15 minutes. Only Corporal Arnold from the 1e, was missing. His mutilated body was found later under a pile of stones.

The companies captured their objectives very quickly: Captain Poulet's 1re reached the Lycée Jean XXIII to the south, Captain Dubos's 2e took over the hospital, whereas Captain Gaussens' 3e took the Impala Hotel and the town centre where it fought off a counter-attack from the Tigers. Two AML-90 (Armoured cars) were captured from the ANC (Cogolese Army) and destroyed by LRAC (Antitanks) shells. The legionaries moved on through a devastated city whose streets were littered with rotting corpses, both white and black. The cellar of Impala Hotel was a charnel house. On the corner of the hotel, twenty severed hands lay on the ground. The Tigers were knocked off balance by the shock of the attack and the

REP sharpshooters worked marvels. Scores of European and African hostages poured out of the houses where they had been hiding and sang the Marseillaise when they saw the paratroopers. Towards 18.00 all the objectives had been reached but the sudden arrival of dusk prevented the second wave from jumping. During the night the rebels tried to infiltrate the French lines but were trapped several times by patrols and legionaries waiting in ambush. At dawn on 20 May the 4e Company jumped in turn to the east of the town. Clearing up operations in the town continued and the legionaries, not the softest of creatures, were nevertheless impressed by the scale and the savagery of the massacres.

In front of the Metal Shaba factory, rebels supported by mortar fire tried to resist. Colonel Erulin entrusted Captain Coevoët with the job of cleaning up this pocket of resistance. The mortars of the REP went into action. The 4e Company held the Tigers while the 2e Company went into the attack. One legionary fell but twenty rebels did not get up off the ground, either. The following days were given over to widening the defensive perimeter and reducing several pockets of resistance.

The rebels seemed to be regrouping in the villages neighbouring Kolwezi. There were therefore operations in the townships of Luilu, Kamoto and Karat from 22-27 May.

By the evening of 28 May the rebels had gone back across the border. The REP had five killed and fifteen wounded. The Tigers left behind them 250 men and a large amount of equipment including two AMLs (Light Amoured car), four SR cannon, fifteen mortars, 21 RPG-7 xxxx and ten heavy machine guns. This was the first operational jump of the French Army since Suez and Algeria and Operation Bonite was particularly well received by public opinion which tended thereafter to magnify the image of the Legion paratrooper.

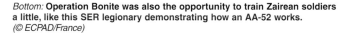

Above and right: **the quantity of weapons taken as booty was impressive; apart from Eastern block weapons coming from Angola with the rebels, the legionaries recovered a lot of Belgian and American weapons abandoned by the fleeing Zairean Army.**
(Kepi Blanc/© ECPAD/France))

Bottom: **Operation Bonite was also the opportunity to train Zairean soldiers a little, like this SER legionary demonstrating how an AA-52 works.**
(© ECPAD/France)

DJIBOUTI

As early as 1974, the 2e REP supplied the 13e DBLE (Foreign Legion Half-Brigade) with a «revolving» company stationed at the *Lieutenant-Colonel Amilakvarit* [1] post at Arta.

The countryside lent itself beautifully to inter-arm exercises as both the Air Force and the Artillery could have a field day and operate for real. For the Legion paratroopers, a tour at Djibouti was a return to sources and reminded them of certain epics of the Legion in the Sahara, with its patrols way into the desert, interminable guard duties right in the middle of the desert and bivouacs in areas which reminded them of the dawn of time. Moreover there was always something going on in the Horn of Africa.

The assault of the Loyada Palm-grove

At the beginning of 1974, the situation in Afar and Issa country was explosive. The country was moving towards independence.

The 13e DBLE increased its patrols in the popular quarters. The 2nd Company of the REP, commanded by Captain Soubirou was on duty in the territory and took part in the operations, one of which was to establish road blocks in order to stop gun smuggling into the town. On 3 February a school bus was captured by seven Issa terrorists which rammed a road block and demanded full independence for Djibouti in exchange for the lives of the thirty-one child hostages. The bus was stopped near the Somali border and negotiations were started between the kidnappers and terrorists who did not hesitate to make the children scream to get what they wanted. With the help of the GIGN (Group d'Intervention de la Gendarmerie Française - French Police Force's Intervention Group), the AML armoured car and the 13e DBLE, Captain Soubirou's 2nd Company, neutralised the terrorists and attacked the Somali frontier post which had been supporting the kidnappers. The seven terrorists were killed and twenty Somali soldiers and rebels neutralised.

An MG-42 machine-gun and several Sturmgeweer rifles were captured but unfortunately two little girls were killed, innocent victims of terrorism. The determination shown by the French soldiers calmed things down a lot and Djibouti became independent calmly. A defence military co-operation agreement enabled France to keep a large garrison there in which the 13e DLBE was the star. During those Cold War years, the strategic situation of that little republic was very important.

On 3 February 1982, there was another drama for the 2e REP in Djibouti when during a jump exercise, a Transall flew into Mount Garbi, killing twenty-five legionaries from the 4e company and two of their officers.

1. One of the Foreign Legion's great figures. This Georgian prince was killed fighting the Afrika Korps in 1942.

Being dragged by the desert wind is a privilege that can only had at the Ambouli Drop Zone near the airport at Djibouti. The fact that they have the use of a Transall means that the 'revolving' company can keep its hand in where airborne operations are concerned.
(Yves Debay)

Right:
'The guard being kept from the top of the crag.' The corrugated roof, sandbags, and above all enough heat to glaze a lizard… Tradition has been respected for this 2e company Legion paratrooper seen in 1988 at Arta
(Yves Debay)

Non-regulation insignia of the 2nd company, 'revolving' in Djibouti in 1975.
(Yves Debay)

Left:
Legionaries preparing their equipment before a jump session. It was during an exercise of this kind that the REP suffered one of its worst tragedies when a Transall crashed into the flanks of Mount Garbi, killing 27 Legion paratroopers of the 4th company
(Yves Debay)

DJIBOUTI

DISCOVERING THE DESERT AGAIN

Myriam firing range caters for all types of weapons and the 'revolving' company takes advantage of it as much as possible. Here a P-4 equipped with a 12.7 mm getting ready to go into action. Chad and Djibouti gave the French Army experience of mechanised desert warfare that few other armies have. *(2e REP archives)*

Above:
**Trudging around the 'Grand Bara', a stone desert
where the temperatures can reach 60°.
The legionaries have abandoned their green beret
and donned their tarbooshes, a rare sight.**
(2e REP archives)

Right:
**First aid exercise. In the wet season,
and in temperatures of 45° with humidity at 95%,
wounds very quickly get worse.**
(© ECPAD/France)

Previous page bottom:
**In the stone setting of Myriam, a platoon has set itself up
under cover, behind a hillock and has fixed the enemy
which a Sagaie armoured car of the 13e DBLE
will try to outflank.**
(Képi Blanc)

A Terrific Training Ground

Apart from the possibility of doing realistic training with live ammunition and carrying out inter-arm manoeuvres without the restrictions which would apply at home, the '*Tournantes*' ('revolving' operations) enabled the companies of the 2e REP to take prt in real operations.

On 17 October 1987, the 3rd Company was engaged in the Ali Sabiegh region against subversive elements which had crossed the border.

From 28 May to 4 June 1991, this same 3rd company was engaged in Operation Godoria which witnessed the disarming of an Ethiopian armoured division which had tried to force the frontier to escape from Eritrean rebels.

Then it was Operation Iskoutir where the 3rd company took part in interposition and humanitarian aid operations in the north of the country from December 1992 to March 1993. The 2nd Company took over this task in March 1993. At the beginning of the 90s, when the Armed Forces were restructured and professionalised the 'revolving' company supplied by the 2e REP was disbanded.

CHAD

FIGHTING IN THE TIBESTI

The photos of the first encounters with the enemy in Chad are rare and of poor quality. Here a column of jeeps is moving northwards.
(Képi Blanc)

There aren't any Jaguars yet… but only some old Skyraiders. After the plane has flown over, the paratroopers will have to search the massif and maybe even fight hand-to-hand with the Toubou rebels.
(Coll. particulière)

Desert and arid mountain ranges to the north, savanna to the south… Warriors believing in the spirit of the forest against the Prophet's horsemen looking for slaves. Sand, blood and a lake which refuses to dry up… that is Chad, the strategic crossroads in the Sahel.

In 1969, President Tombalbaye had asked France to respect its defence agreements and fight the FROLINAT… It was the beginning of an adventure which lasted thirty years for the French Troops, who were faced with different factions against a background of ethnic conflicts and open intervention on the part of Libya.

It was in April 1969 that 390 men, principally Legion paratroopers and a few Red Berets, landed at Fort-Lamy which was not yet called N'Djamena. These men formed the EMT 1 *(Etat-Major Tactique N°1/Tactical Headquarters N°1)* under the command of Major de Chastenet. The unit was mainly made up of 2e REP soldiers, namely two combat companies, one mortar platoon and a command element and services.

Equipped with old Dodges and jeeps dating back to WWII, the legionaries looked as though they were back in Algeria. They were armed almost the same, with an MAS semi-automatic rifle and the famous MAT-49 Machine Pistol. The men wore safari hats and adopted the khaki tarboosh which was indispensable in this semi-desert terrain. Sometimes an old Sikorsky S-58 flew over the columns as they

moved in a northerly direction in a hellish cloud of dust.

EMT 1 set up its headquarters in Mangalmé from which motorised detachments drove out so as *'to be seen'*. On 29 April, Captain Milin was severely ambushed. For the first time, the legionaries met a new adversary which they learned to respect: the Goran or Tubu warrior, tall, thin, very rustic and knowing the lie of the land very well. Two assault groups of two hundred men armed with assegais but led by a dozen armed individuals went into the attack. The heights were protected by support groups and the commander gave his orders from a distance with a whistle.

During the whole period of the engagement, a radio network transmitted in Russian and co-ordinated the rebels' action. Lieutenant Germanos, the future boss of the 11e DP got his group out of the situation. No casualties for the Legion, but the rebels had lost fifty-odd killed.

For six months, EMT 1 wandered around the sumptuous Tibesti countryside. By truck except where the rainy season forbade their use; then it was on horseback.

At Mangalmé, Lieutenant Pietri had formed a local mounted detachment which took part in the operations. The frequent sallies made by the legionaries was beginning to get results, especially with the help of the Sikorskys from the ALAT *(Aviation légère de l'Armée de Terre/Army Air Corps)*.

Right:
A pause in the savannah, no doubt during the move northwards, in 1969. Chad was naturally a quiet front and equipment was at first particularly obsolete like these old Dodge trucks.
(Képi Blanc)

Au centre:
During the Tibesti operations, the Sikorsky S-58 returned to operations and faced the desert wind again, ten years after Algeria.
(Képi Blanc)

Bottom:
Legion paratroopers in Chad in 1970. The uniforms and weapons are those that were used in Algeria. The jungle hat was typical of the period.
(Képi Blanc)

EMT 1 did some clearing up at Bitkine, Eref and Niegui and especially Massaloua where sixty-eight rebels bit the dust.

However, the Chad Army's incapacity to deal with the crisis and Libya's increasing aid to the rebels made the operations more and more difficult. The arrival of reinforcements was vital.

A second EMT as formed and in October 1969, the 2e REP at full strength reinforced with the CMLE *(Compagnie motorisée de la Légion Etrangère/Motorised Company of the Foreign Legion)* supplied by 1st Etranger, was in Chad under the command of Colonel Lacaze. Encounters with the remarkable Tubu warriors became more frequent and intense, but everywhere the Legionaries were getting results, especially during Operation Cantharide during which order was restored in the Tibesti which enabled economic activity to start up again.

On 13 February 1970, Lieutenant Pietri's 'cavalry' escorting the Mangalmé Sous-Préfet on an administrative tour 'encountered' and put 11 rebels out of action.

In March, the 1st company was operating with the Chadian Nomad Guards. On 6 March in the Ouaddai, the two units were in contact with a strong band of rebels. Hurrying under fire to the help of a wounded Chadian adjudant, Médecin-Capitaine de Larrez de la Dorie was mortally wounded.

In April 1970, France started to disengage itself from Chad, but EMT 2 and Major Malaterre's CMLE stayed and distinguished themselves in the Zouar region where the situation was getting increasingly bad. On 22 October in the Leclerc fault, Captain Wabinski's company had gone to gather in the terrified men from two Chadian outposts which had fallen back into a narrow defile.

The fighting was deadly and lasted 36 hours. The legionaries were slightly exposed and had to face determined Tubu warriors, hidden in the rocks and armed with rifles with eyesights. The legionaries manoeuvred, searched the caves and after combing throughtthe rocks were masters of the field at the price of one killed and seven wounded. Forty rebels were killed.

A last large-scale operation resulted in another two killed and twelve wounded at Fada in the Malaterre group which put a group of fifty rebels out of action.

On 20 December 1970, the last legionaires left this legendary country. They would be back.

CHAD

OPERATION TACAUD

In 1978, Operation *Tacaud 4* meant that the French were again involved in fighting against the GUNT bands of Goukouni Oueddei, supported by Libya.

For a while, elements of the 2e REP under the command of Lieutenant-Colonel Lhopitalier organised a training course for the Chadian army. This small 30-strong detachment was only to take part in the fighting only if absolutely necessary, i.e. a direct threat to N'Djamena. The times had really changed since 1969 and now Jaguars and Pumas were there able to give air support.

They were engaged alongside the *Tacaud 4* detachment during the fighting at Barangue where the rebels lost fifty or so men.

On 19 May, on the same day as the operation over Kolwezi, elements of the 2e REP supporting the Chadians took part in the battle of Ati with the 3e RIMa. This was a serious business and the rebels were no longer equipped with assegais. As well as the 70 men they left behind them on the field, the rebels abandoned sixty weapons among which two mortars, one 81 and one 120 mm, one 14.5 mm KPV twin-tube, six machine-guns, 2 RPG-7s and twenty assault rifles. The Chadians in the REP learnt their lesson well and a few days later in the Djedaa palm-grove they destroyed the remainder of the fugitives from Ati with the help of the 3e RPIMa and a squadron of the 1er REC *(Régiment étranger de Cavalerie/Foreign Legion Cavalry Regiment)*.

CHAD

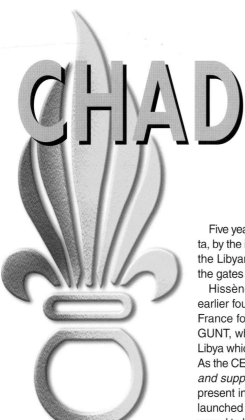

OPERATION MANTA

Five years later in June 1983, it was Operation Manta, by the impact of its mere presence, which enabled the Libyans to be pushed back when they reached the gates of N'Djamena.

Hissène Habre, the new president who had earlier fought the French, nevertheless appealed to France for help to drive back Goukouni Oueddei's GUNT, which was openly armed and supported by Libya which itself had engaged troops in the fighting. As the CEA *(Compagnie d'éclairage et d'appui/Scout and support company)* of the 2e REP was already present in N'Djamena on a 'revolving' basis, France launched Operation *Manta*. The operation was supposed to be first and foremost one of dissuasion, the Chadians doing all the fighting with the French doing all the logistics, and only intervening if the 16th Parallel was crossed. The warning to Gaddafi was clear.

The 2e REP took part in Operation Manta from November 1983 to May 1984. It was the Corps Commander, Lieutenant-Colonel Janvier who took command of the Manta-Echo detachment which operated out of Biltine. The 2e REP was 1 026 strong and with the exception of the 4th Company based at Ati, it radiated out into the Biltine, Arada, Abéché and Irida sectors. Apart from his Legion paratroopers. Colonel Janvier also received the support of an artillery battery composed of an HM-2 howitzer and a squadron of AML-90s.

Right:
1984 Captain Guermeur's company patrolling in the region of Ati is not faraway. Operation *Tacaud*'s jungle hat has been replaced by the green beret. The enemy has to know that the Foreign Legion has arrived.
(© ECPAD/France)

Centre:
Everything seems to indicate that the Gunts are nearby, particularly this recently-placed anti-personnel mine which these Chad auxiliaries have brought to the legionaries.
(© ECPAD/France)

Left:
**Watching and waiting south of the 16th parallel…
This legionary of the 1^e company is probably in the Tatar desert.**
(ECPA)

43

CHAD

OPERATION MANTA

In January 1984, Captain Fraye's 3rd company, 'revolving' in the Central African Republic, rejoined *Manta-Echo*. The press liked to compare Operation *Manta* with the situation in the *'Tartar desert'* where, out in the empty terrain, men waited for an enemy who was present but whom they never saw. Even if the outposts in Chad did resemble those of the Legion in the Sahara and even if the mission was similar, the detachments on the spot were not inactive and patrolled around endlessly.

Next to the old jeeps and GMCs, the Legion Paratroopers had more modern equipment such as Mira cameras, Milan radios which help with the shooting but also with night observation.

Difficulties concerning the more than difficult living conditions were a challenge to the legionaries' ingenuity and resourcefulness… After having 'swallowed up kilometre after kilometre of dirt track and dust', the *Béret Vert* would always find a small mess where he could get a Galla, the famous Chadian beer. All the soldiers, journalists or mere simple civilians who have passed through Chad have heard of Father Lallemand, the 2e REP's almoner who devoted part of his life to the Chadians. He became the almoner to the Chadian Army, and he did not hesitate to travel thousands of kilometres by himself in the middle of Muslim country to celebrate mass.

After a few timid reconnaissances along the 16th Parallel, Gaddafi and his allies no longer sought direct confrontation with the French forces. After six months spent on the Echo axis, the 2e REP returned home to Calvi.

ECS Biltine insigna.

CHAD

OPERATION EPERVIER

Epervier (Sparrowhawk) followed *Manta*. The set up was almost the same since Libya was threatening its southern neighbour once again. From Bouar in the Central African Republic, Colonel Germanos sent the 3rd and 4th Companies into Chad. They were included in the dispositions around N'Djamena airport.

From May 1986, *Epervier* was above all an aerial contingent base, Mirages and Jaguars refuelled by KC-135s bombing the northern bases whereas Hawk missiles shot down two marauding Tupolev 22s. The principal mission of the Legion Paratroopers was to guard the airport. In May 1987, an EMT *(Etat-Major Tactique/Tactical Headquarters)* under the command of Colonel Wabinski replaced the land part

Below.
A Foreign Legion column enters Biltine, the most important French Army post in Chad...
After kilometres of tracks, these legionaries will probably have an ice-cold Gala (beer).
(© ECPAD/France)

The arrival of Ilyushin Il-76 'Candid' heavy transport planes, come to take prisoners away, takes place under heavy guard.
(© ECPAD/France)

2nd REP insigna
for Operation Epervier.

of *Epervier* with four companies. The locations were already familiar names and were seen again with pleasure by the veterans: Kalait, Biltine and Abéché. Hissène Habré's big victories at Fada, Ouadi-Doum and Faya-Largeau enabled the contingent to be reduced. Nevertheless the 2e REP was accustomed to the *Epervier* mission because it was frequently deployed.

In order not to increase tension in the North, the 'revolving' units were based at Dubut Camp at N'Djamena.

Abéché, the new home

From October 1988 to March 1989 under the command of Colonel Coevoët, the 2e REP was in Chad. The regiment carried out a number of incursions into the south and left several detachments at important sites like Abéché, the starting point for all operations towards the north.

In November 1990, the 2nd, 3rd and 4th companies and the CRAP group under the command of

Colonel Gausserès, had to intervene to protect foreigners and installations when Idriss Deby seized power.

The REP companies occupied the key points of the Chadian capital which was in complete chaos. On several occasions the Legion paratroopers opened fire to chase away bands of looters or to disarm threatening groups. 1 600 foreigners of all nationalities including Libyan prisoners were evacuated. The regiment came back to Chad two months later as part of a normal tour of duty, the tenth time since 1969.

In 1992, after the regiment had been relieved in June, the 2nd company returned to Abéché in December to counter the activities of Hissène Habré's partisans who were starting trouble.

On 2 January, taking advantage of the passage of the Paris-Dakar rally, an armed band took over the hamlets of Liwa and Bol, thereby threatening N'Djamena. Part of the 2nd company was flown in. The mere sight of the Berets Verts brought calm back to the town.

After three year's absence, the 2e REP returned to Chad under the command of Colonel Poulet.

Apart from the operational aspects and the fact of being in the heart of the action, a posting to Chad was always appreciated by the French soldiers because the climate, the setting and the space enabled them to train in situations which closely resembled reality and which are impossible to realise in Europe because of over-stringent security measures.

The desert wind marks the men and forges their character… this type of authentic country can only be appreciated by the Legion paratroopers.

LEBANON

In August 1982, 10 000 well-armed Palestinians were blocked in Beirut facing two divisions and four armoured brigades of the Israeli Army. The ALP (Palestine Liberation Army) and other left-wing Lebanese militias were supporting them with of 6 000 fighting men.

The Syrian Army which also had elements in Beirut was ready to intervene from its bases in the Bekaa Valley with six brigades and especially 80 brand-new T-72s. The Lebanese powder barrel was on the point of exploding but, under the command of Colonel Janvier, the 2e REP contributed to putting out the fuse. The Habib plan was the last chance providing for the evacuation of the PLO from the Lebanon.

Operation Epaulard was one of the military parts and from the 17 August, the 2e REP was on Leopard alert (code name for the highest leval alert). Within the dispositions of the multinational intervention force, grouping Italian, French and American soldiers, the 2e REP was entrusted with the safety of the Palestinians who were evacuating their positions in Beirut.

Starting in Cyprus, the legionaries boarded the logistics supply vessel Rance and the tank transporter *Dives*. On 20 August, the convoy escorted by the frigates *Dupleix* and *Georges Leygue* headed for the Lebanese coast. The aircraft carrier Foch, the companion of crisis days and the ships of the US 6th Fleet ensured that there was air cover. Captain Puga's 1st Company was first off the Dives followed by the 3rd to control the port.

The sections moved forward through an apocalyptic landscape; tension mounted when Lieutenant Guermeur was faced with soldiers from Tsahal who did not want to evacuate their positions. At 7 a.m. on 20 August, the port was in French hands.

71 Palestinians with their arms and luggage were escorted before leaving for Tunis via Cyprus. In indescribable bedlam, punctuated by rifle shots, the trucks bearing Palestinian colours and full to bursting with men wearing kefiehs, the famous

Joint Franco-Lebanese guard near the Résidence des Pins at Baabda. Below the legionary, the Lebanese post with a Saladin armoured car.
(© ECPAD/France)

LEBANON

RESCUE ARAFAT!

head-dress and carrying Kalashnikovs left for yet another exile. Impassive, the legionaries made sure that nothing got out of hand.

On 30 August it was Yasser Arafat's turn to leave. He was protected by the CRAP until he boarded the Atlantis. When it was known to what extent the Leader of the PLO's life was in danger, the choice-of the 2e REP's CRAPs for this last escort mission was a very wise one.

From the 26 August, the US Marines relieved the REP in the port. The regimental command post was installed in the French Embassy, the famous 'Residence des Pins', whereas the legionaries took over the positions on the green line abandoned by the Palestinians and the Syrians.

The legionaries discovered, not without surprise and admiration, the complexity of the Palestinian fortified system on Omar-Beyhum Square.

Each house was a blockhaus with booby-trapped access and fall-back paths. In order to get hold of this complex, held by 400 Fedayeens, the Tsahal would have had to pay a heavy price by forcing its

way through a bloody labyrinth of trap doors, traps, remote controlled rockets and other mines.

On 26 August, from new positions in town, the 3rd company escorted the Syrian 'Hittine' division on its way to Damascus, before handing the positions over to the Lebanese Army.

President Gemayel was disappointed when the legionaries returned to Calvi on 13 September 1982. Operation Epaulard was a complete success and all the press was unanimous in praising the behaviour of the Legion paratroopers.

Next page
Beirut, 1982, the Green Line.
(© ECPAD/France)

Next page top:
Picture of an evacuation… the REP keeping an eye out for trouble. The legionaries' calm contrasts with the very oriental exuberance of the crowd.
(© ECPAD/France)

Next page centre:
The 1e company escorting twin-cannon 23 mm BTR-152s probably belonging to the Syrian army.
(© ECPAD/France)

Below:
A PLO jeep drives past two legionaries on guard along one of Beirut's main thoroughfares. The tricolour armband appeared during Epaulard, and was seen again at Sarajevo and other interposition missions.
(© ECPAD/France)

GABON

OPERATION REQUIN

bottom:

A legionary from the 2nd company guarding the French Embassy in Libreville during Operation *Requin* (Shark)
(© ECPAD/France)Right:

1. **Training doesn't stop.**
   (Képi Blanc)
2. **Securing the airport.**
   (Képi Blanc)
3. **A Urutu government armoured vehicle.**
   (© ECPAD/France)

In March 1990, President Bongo's authority was widely contested. Port-Gentil, the economic capital of Gabon and the opposition stronghold, was on the verge of rebellion. This broke out two months later. In this oil town, the 6 000 French residents were under threat, when the trouble reached Libreville.

The French consul was taken hostage for a while. France decided to send in the forces already in situ and in Central Africa to evacuate the French nationals but also to protect its oil investments.

At Calvi, Captain Lieutaud's 2nd company was on *Leopard alert*. At 14.00, on 24 May, the 'Reds' took off to rejoin the Marine (Navy) paratroopers and a company of the 2e REI. First, the legionaries ensured that the French Embassy was safe.

Faced with the seriousness of the situation, the Quai d'Orsay decided to evacuate some of the nationals. On 27 May, the 2nd company went off into the jungle and started bringing in the French and other foreign residents from Lambaréné and Rabi-Kounda. Then it stayed in Port-Gentil as a dissuasion. The 2nd company was entrusted with the protection of the airport and was kept in reserve.

As was often the case in *Black' Africa*, the outburst of violence which was severely repressed by the Gabonese army was only a flash in the pan. Before going home, the Legion paratroopers took the time to recover by using the famous Malibé ground at the *Centre d'Entrainement Commando* - the African forest commando training centre.

IRAQ

In August 1990, Saddam Hussein invaded Kuwait. France joined its traditional allies to restore Kuwait's sovereignty. This was Operation *Daguet*.

On 9 February, under the command of Colonel Rosier, the 1er RPIMa Corps Commander, the CRAPs of the 11e DP regrouped at Toulouse before moving off to Riyadh. On the 13th, having spotted some VLRAs, they deployed at al Rafah where they prepared for land operations.

They crossed the border on 23 February. The NBC *(Nucléaire-Bactériologique-Chimique/Nuclear-Bacteriological-Chemical)* 1 alert level explained why elite soldiers who normally try to lessen the weight that they carry, were wearing heavy anti-gas uniforms. Having progressed along the Beaulieu axis with the 1er Spahis, the CRAPs attacked an ammunition dump near al Salman, capturing several 1,405 mm cannon. On 26 February, at the head of the *Daguet* division, the CRAPs got hold of Fort al Salman. A cluster bomb was accidentally set off killing two soldiers and wounding twenty-five others, among which two CRAPs from the 2e REP.

A last helicopter operation was aimed at a radio relaying station at Al Shabkha. With the ALAT's HOT Gazelles, the commandos destroyed the antennae with MILANs and brought back 90 prisoners.

Above:
One of the most well-known photos of the Gulf War: the 2e REP CRAPs at Fort Al-Salman. Note the NBC uniform and the doubling up of the weapons: MP-5 and FAMAS.
(2e REP archives)

Left:
A VLRA loaded with 11e DP CRAPs moving on during a sand storm; a large part of Operation *Daguet* was carried out in very bad weather conditions. The VLRA is so perfectly adapted to this type of mission t hat the famous British SAS have ordered them.
(© ECPAD/France)

OPERATION NOROÎT

RWANDA

The Tutsis' homecoming after the massacres of 1959 sparked off a civil war in Rwanda which marked the end of the Hutus' hold on the country, but also a new form of destabilisation on the African continent where particularly French interests were particularly threatened. In October 1990, the French government, after consulting the Belgians, launched Operation Noroit, aimed at ensuring the protection and the evacuation of European nationals.

'Revolving' in Central Africa, the CRAPs and the 4th company moved towards Kigali where they occupied several regrouping points and the airport.

The legionaries were shot at several times by snipers but they did not shoot back, and by their mere presence brought order back to the town. After a ten-month stay, the 4th company returned to Calvi where several legionaries were awarded the croix de la valeur militaire (*Military Valour Cross*).

On 4 November, the Legion paratroopers came back to the *'Country of a thousand hills'* as part of the Operation *Noroit* contingent.

From November 1991 to March 1992, the 3rd company and an EMT were deployed in this superb country still a prey of tribalism. Its mission was to protect European nationals among which 60 French people and to prepare them for a possible evacuation.

Within the framework of the DAMI *(Détachement d'Assistance Militaire - the Military Assistance Detachment)*, the REP supplied technical advisors to the Rwandan Army which was facing a push from the FPR (Rwanda Popular Front) Front coming from Uganda. *Noroit* was supposed to be a discreet operation and in theory France was not supposed to join in the fighting.

It followed developments very closely. In this context and despite heightened tension, the sections started reconnaissance operations which enabled them to measure the gravity of the situation. On 19 February, in the Galo region the captain's 4 x 4 P-4 vehicle was following a minibus which blew up on a land-mine a few kilometres from where the legionaries were stationed.

On 26 February after an alert, the Berets Verts arrived on the scene of a massacre, nine Rwandan civilians and an old white nun had been executed by the rebels. I March 1992, the detachment was relieved by other great soldiers, the 'paras-colos' of the 3e RPIMa *(Colonial Parachute regiment)*.

Given the degree of secrecy attached to Operation *Noroit*, photographs are rare and not very good.

The DAMI inaction with the FAR (Forces Armées Rwandaises - Rwandan armed forces).
(Képi Blanc.)

The REP was entrusted with training the soldiers engaged in the struggle against the FPR,

as this movement was supported by the Ugandan government, Anglo-Saxon mercenaries also gave technical assistance to the Tutsi rebels.
(Képi Blanc)

An officer from the 3rd company giving help to the Rwandans setting up a MILAN firing position on a Rwandan army VBL
(3e compagnie)

OPERATION TURQUOISE

In April 1994, President Habyarimana was killed in an attack on his plane, which was bringing him back from Burundi; this gave the signal for the extermination of the Tutsis organised by Hutu extremists against the Tutsis.

At the same time, the FPR, made up of Tutsis and supported by Uganda launched a huge offensive with a view to taking power. All the African Lakes area looked likely to flare up.

On 22 June 1994 it was estimated that there been 500 000 people had been massacred, hundreds of thousands of refugees had fled to Zaire where a cholera epidemic broke out. The United Nations gave France the green light to go ahead with a humanitarian relief programme whilst waiting for the deployment of troops from *MINUAR II.* 2 500 French soldiers took part in Operation *Turquoise* which aimed at establishing a safe zone for the humanitarian operation.

This operation was very controversial but it nevertheless enabled 20 000 Tutsi refugees to be saved. Among the French troops which already included the COS (Commandement des Opérations Spéciales - Special Operations Command), a group of Marines and a group from the Legion, there were the CRAPs of the 2e REP. The CRAPs pursued looters, disarmed deserting Rwandan soldiers, countered infiltration by the FPR and supervised the the new police force within the humanitarian perimeter.

SOMALIA OPERATION ORYX

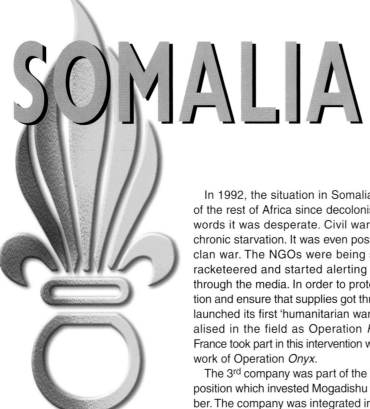

In 1992, the situation in Somalia reflected that of the rest of Africa since decolonisation. In other words it was desperate. Civil war was added to chronic starvation. It was even possible to call it a clan war. The NGOs were being systematically racketeered and started alerting public opinion through the media. In order to protect the population and ensure that supplies got through, the USA launched its first 'humanitarian war' which materialised in the field as Operation *Restore Hope*. France took part in this intervention within the framework of Operation *Onyx*.

The 3rd company was part of the impressive disposition which invested Mogadishu from 9 December. The company was integrated into the Marines Expeditionary Forces of the USMC. Rubbing shoulders with the 'Leather Necks', and in the media limelight, the sections controlled several of the big roads in and out of town. At 20.30 the 1st platoon was attacked and replied in order to disengage itself.

Supported by the LVTP -7s and the LAVs of the USMC, the Legion paratroopers controlled access to the town for several days.

The positions were often harassed and on 10 December, a vehicle forced a road block causing the legionaries to open fire on it.

An American armoured vehicle opened fire on the platoon and its command post without, fortunately, hitting anybody. During the following days, the Marines and the legionaries worked together, taking Baidoa and recovering a large quantity of equipment, including D-30 howitzers and vehicles armed with 23 mm twin-barrels. On 20 December, two sections took part in a night ambush where the COS was attacked. From 25 December, the 3rd company let the Americans to join the *BAT 13* made up of the 13e DBLE.

The 3rd company remained one more month in Somalia, escorting humanitarian convoys before leaving the country.

Above
**FR-F2 Sniper in position
in the streets of Mogadishu,
during the first days of the operation.
As often during operations
in the Third World, the presence
of people everywhere
can turn out to be a real nuisance,
particularly when there is shooting.**
(© ECPAD/France)

Inset:
**During a tense moment,
a legionary gets ready
to use a rifle** *(© ECPAD/France)*

Rght:
**Two 3rd company legionaries
meet a Marine Corps LAV light
armoured vehicle and a captured
'technical' car.**
(© ECPAD/France)

Previous page:
**In the heat, the 'Blacks'
control the key points
of Mogadishu.
Note below, the American
amphibious LVTP-7
armoured vehicle.**
(© ECPAD/France)

BOSNIA

In 1991, for the first time since 1945, war returned to Europe when ex-Yugoslavia flared up. In the spring of 1992, the fighting which had until then been confined to Croatia, spread to neighbouring Bosnia. In order to try and defuse this more-than-explosive situation and by means of resolution 743, the UN commissioned an international force, the FORPRONU, to supervise a cease-fire between the Croats and the Serbs.

Further resolutions authorised an increase in the size of the force which was also deployed in Bosnia. President Mitterand's visit to Sarajevo in June 1992 enabled an airlift to be set up to relieve the population. But the siege was not finished for all that. Sarajevo and its suburbs saw French-bat (French battalion) attempting to carry out interposition missions and to escort humanitarian convoys to the

devastated civilian population as best it could. Very often, the powerless French troops could only count the blows. The mission was too vague since their restrained response was not adapted to this situation against militias who only respected force and continued to increase their shooting to intimidate and harass. Contradictory orders from the UN did not make matters any simpler.

It was in this context that the 2e REP replaced troops, trained as they were to manoeuvre and charge ahead.

Here it was exactly the opposite. Well dug in and wearing those very thick anti-shrapnel jackets, they had to remain aloof and ignore all sorts of provocation, and take mortar fire and shots from snipers who knew they would go unpunished… that was what a UN mission was like. The legionaries car-

ried it out with exemplary coolness. Knowing that they were vastly superior to the rabble who opposed them on the front lines at Butmir and Illidza, on either side of the airport, they were happy just to smile scornfully in reply to a bullet which had just hit the parapet or crazed the windscreen in front of them. Legionary Mark Kay was thus wounded twice in less than three months.

On 16 January 1993, the battalion was complete and under the command of Colonel Poulet which had the 1st, the 4th companies reinforced by elements from the CCS (compagnie de commande-ment de service/Command and services Compa-ny), from the 17ᵉ RGP *(Régiment de Génie para-chutiste/Parachute Engineer Regiment)* and 14ᵉ RPCS *(Regiment parachutiste de commandement et de soutien/Parachute)*. Its principal mission was to hold the airport and protect the distribution of humanitarian aid. A part of the CEA joined them later. the EMT of the RICM *(Régiment d'infanterie colonial mixte/Mixt colonial infantry Regiment)* in Sarajevo on 13 December 1993. For the first time the Berets Verts exchanged their hats for the Blue Berets. It was a delicate mission for these shock.

SARAJEVO

THE FORTRESS AIRPORT

Ever since the airport was back in service in July 1992, the security perimeter around the buildings and the runways were littered with control points, command and observation posts all built up by the Coloniale.

The Legion improved on them, even starting a quarry within the airport for filling sandbags. From the fortress airport the legionaries had a front seat for watching the daily fighting between Bosnians and Croats. *'What are our cousins going to do today?'* the president of the NCOs would repeat

daily; he was himself of Yugoslav origin. Helmets and bullet-proof jackets were worn all the time because mortar shots very often fell short on the car park… intentionally or not.

After a mission to Butmir where the REP carried out the evacuation of a young woman and her newborn baby, legionary Ratislav Benko of the 1st company was killed by Bosnian mortar fire directed wittingly at the airport car park.

The shot came from Butmir…

Bottom:
For the REP, the first UNO mission was an opportunity to get to know the equipment of the ex-'enemies' in the Warsaw pact. Here French VABs meet Ukrainian BTR-70s on the tarmac.
(Yves Debay)

Bottom:
The airport at Sarajevo was the town's only link with the outside world. The air bridge was kept up during the whole siege. An REP 20 mm canon-equipped VAB protects the standstill point of an Ilyushin Il-70 'Candid'.
(J.Y. Kerbrat)

Above
In a few months the airport at Sarajevo was changed into a real dug-in camp, surrounded everywhere by the front line.
(Yves Debay)

AGAINST THE SNIPERS

There was another danger: the snipers who either under orders or under the influence of Slivovitch - plum brandy - took pot shots at the positions. In order to counter this threat, the REP formed 'counter-sniping' groups which were perfectly hidden and who had noted all the enemy positions by means of teamwork and a long time spent on observation… if necessary they could pull the trigger of their FR-F2s.

Another thankless task but which was made easier by MIRA cameras, was chasing civilian and military Bosnians who tried during the night to use the airport perimeter to leave or to supply Sarajevo. As the UN was neutral this was not tolerated and moreover the Serbs would let loose at the airport runways with all they had if they once suspected something was afoot.

During one of these missions, in the night of 1 June, two legionaries were seriously wounded by bullets, bringing to 28 the number of wounded among the soldiers of Frenchbat.

**These two shots show a sniper's lair,
set up in one of the buildings at Sarajevo airport.
A young English legionary has taken up position
with his FR-F2. Hidden by an old blanket,
the position is invisible from the outside.
All the potential enemy sniper hideouts
have been catalogued
on the panoramic photo in the lair.
Thanks to the Motorola walky-talky,
our sniper is in contact
with other similar positions.**
(Yves Debay)

BOSNIA

At Sarajevo, the 2ᵉ REP was transformed into motorised infantry for the first time, which was a natural move in the 11ᵉ DP seeing as, even in Africa, firepower had increased considerably with the massive arms sales from the ex- Warsaw Pact countries' stocks.

But at Sarajevo, the white VAB (armed personnel Carrier) were used particularly as taxis for important UN civil servants or as transport for supplies, water, medicines to the affected quarters. The convoys often came under fire from isolated marksmen or stopped by local, finicky 'small fry' bosses with whom they had to negotiate their right to pass without ever forcing things. That was the rule of the UN.

Bottom:
'It's for them that we're here'. Contact between the legionaries and the children is always good; here the chocolate ration will no doubt shortly change hands!
(Yves Debay)

LESSONS TO BE LEARNT

Legion paratroopers in Sarajevo airport car park, at the very spot where they lost one of their own, and where many others would be wounded.
(Yves Debay)

With hindsight, it is naturally easy to criticise the role of the UN at Sarajevo and to compare its apparently pointless activity with that of the IFOR three years later.

Nevertheless, the participants cannot be taken to task the presence of the REP certainly enabled dozens of lives to be saved. It doubtless easier for a soldier to go into the attack than not to react when faced with men who shoot at him whilst he's feeding their children.

The Legion paratroopers' calm and nerves of stee -even the youngest were used to gunfire now - enabled them to return to Calvi after a new experience in July 1993. Colonel Sarthe who commanded the French bat before the arrival of the REP declared *'Sarajevo, the French battalion which loved you passionately, will cry when it leaves you, but it will depart without any illusions.'*

Bottom:
A supply mission to Butmir. To reach this village, situated on the other side of the airport runway, the legionaries have to cross the lines twice at great risk.
(Yves Debay)

BOSNIA

2nd REP-IFOR insigna

Patrolling one of Mount Igman's tracks in the snow. The 2nd company is in its element.
(Képi Blanc)

In Autumn 1995, the 2ᵉ REP got ready to leave for Bosnia again, under the orders of Colonel Darry. But this time things had at last changed and it was as the relief for the FFR that the regiment was engaged. After the hostage crisis and the capture of Vrbanja Bridge, Great Britain, the Netherlands and France created the FRR *(Force de Reaction Rapide - Rapid Reaction Force.)* which was immediately engaged on Mount Igman to alleviate the Serb stranglehold on Sarajevo.

To the Force's artillery were soon added NATO backed air raids. This show of strength, under the command of General Soubirou, a former REP man, ended by bringing the belligerents to the negotiating table and contributed to lifting the siege of Sarajevo. In the cold and the snow the 2ᵉ REP set itself up on Mount Igman and on the crests overlooking the Neretva.

On 20 December, authority was transferred and the regiment came under NATO control. Its mission was to watch over the implementation of the Dayton Agreement. The Legion paratroopers exchanged their UN blue berets with some relief for their green ones. It was no longer a matter of humming and hawing; at the first sign of resistance, the legionaries set themselves up in combat positions whilst NATO aircraft flew around in the sky. The IFOR (Implementation Force) which had replaced FOR-PRONU, did not have the same weaknesses. The

2nd, 3rd and 4th companies emptied dozens of positions of their former occupants with the CEA pointing its 120 mm mortar barrels at them.

The 2ᵉ company had the opportunity to demonstrate its mountain speciality when it was engaged on Mount Igman. In two metres of snow, living in freezing shelters, patrolling on skis or snowshoes showed that the training in the Alps had borne its fruits. The 4e company carried out an armoured raid on Goradze to demonstrate that the IFOR had a totally free rein.

The 5th company had a lot on its plate supporting all these people and gave of itself entirely when the Neretva burst its banks and flooded the Vrapcici quarter. The 2ᵉ REP's EMT could also count on a squadron of AMX-10RC (Heavy Armoured Car) from the 1ᵉʳ REC and on the parachute sappers from the 17ᵉ RGP, who were always present where there was trouble.

Operation *'Aigle Noir'* (Black Eagle) had the CRAPs transported by Blackhawk helicopters of the US Special Forces, in order to invest an islamic training centre and a large stock of weapons was captured.

The regiment returned to Calvi in April 1996 to celebrate Camerone Day. The winter of 1995-96 was an enriching experience for the REP because the regiment had proved that it operate in a winter and under operational conditions.

Right
During their stay in Bosnia under the colours of the IFOR, the legionaries took control of dozens of positions abandoned by the belligerents. Here the 'Repmen' are emptying a Serb M-47 tank of its ammunition.
(Archives 2e REP)

Right
IFOR is not FORPRONU and any attempts at resistance are dealt with by force. The CEA 12 mm mortars have taken up position on Mount Igman. In the VABs, the ammunition is not for exercise.
(Képi Blanc)

Bottom:
Driving on ice is not always easy and it doesn't always help being motorised, viz. this VAB.
(Képi Blanc)

C.A.R.

CHECKING A MUTINY: OPERATION ALMANDIN

Once again, the eastern part of the Central African Republic at the beginning of spring 1996 looked like a tropical caldron. Against a background of tribal strife between Saras, Mbakas and Yako- mas, the struggle for power was intensifying. Part of the army which was mainly Yakoma (5% of the CAR's population), accepted the president's author- ity with difficulty.

Ange Patassé, a Sara, had been elected demo- cratically but his running of the government was leading the country towards a catastrophe. The president 'forgot' to pay the army which mutinied three times. French soldiers from the EFAO (Elé- ments Français d'Assistance Operationelle - French Operational Help Elements) intervened the first time in April 1996 so that the confrontation between the

presidential guard and the Army did not turn into a massacre. In November 1996, the third mutiny broke out; this was in fact military sedition.

The mutineers at Camp Kasai had most of the advantages as they held almost all the CAR's heavy armament and had the support of the Yakoma pop- ulation in the Bimbo, Bakongo and Kouanga quar- ters, which enabled them to hold the town centre in a pincer movement.

Faced with the gravity of the situation, France reacted and the reinforcements started to arrive with the increase in tension. These included the 3rd and 4th companies of the 2e REP, detached from their Epervier mission in Chad. Under the command of Colonel Puga, they made up an EMT *(Etat-major Tactique/Tactical headquarters)* Nord. On

30 December 1996, the mutineers used crowd movements to try and get into the town centre. The riot lasted two days. The sector was held by the 'Colos' who had to fire in the air and pull back several times to avoid a blood-bath.

The turbulent Yakoma started up all over again on 4 January 1997 and with arrows and Molotov cocktails attacked the Marsouins (Marines) who were trying to open up Avenue Boganda, the main axis of Bangui. Accompanied by two officers from the 6e RPIMa, the African officers from the 'comité de suivi' — the follow-up liaison committee — tried to negotiate with the demonstrators.

Suddenly two men jumped out from the crowd and shot the two French officers in the back. A platoon from the 2e REP intervened to free the African officers.

Ever since the Vrbanja Bridge affair, the political authorities in France have refused to tolerate the humiliation and the murder of French soldiers. So the operation to bring back law and order began in the night of 4-5 January.

The COS (Commandement de Opérations Spéciales/Special Operations Command) to which the GCP of the REP belonged, got itself into Bimbo, whereas the 3rd and 4th companies and the 2nd company of the 8e RPIMa started a vast combing operation. The operation was supported by a canon-equipped Puma from the COS which turned out to be very effective. There were a few skirmishes but in the night-fighting the mutineers were just not good enough.

At dawn, the rebel quarters had been calmed down, a dozen or so mutineers had been killed, twenty captured and the Legion paratroopers were able to display two heavy machine guns and some captured vehicles.

It was true that the population remained hostile, but the return of law and order encouraged economic activity to take up again and confidence was restored. In order to patrol in the former rebel quarters, the Legion paratroopers put aside their burst-proof jackets and heavy helmets. The children started asking for presents again and negotiations started again. Almandin 2 no doubt saved the CAR from civil war.

Nevertheless several more incidents occurred. On 10 January, a platoon of the 4th company commanded by Captain Talbourdel prevented armed civilians from racketeering the local population. A man was shot dead by a corporal after wounding a legionary.

On 16 January, the 3rd company had an 'encounter' with some mutineers at the N'diri crossroads, on the road to Camp Kasai. An encounter between two patrols caused a sharp exchange of fire. The mutineers fell back, covered by mortar fire, leaving one dead and one prisoner in the hands of the legionaries.

Operation Almandin 2 enabled a climate of security to be created which allowed a pan-African force to be deployed in order to check on the application of the agreement between rival Central African brothers.

Top:
On the roof of the TELECOM centre, on the outskirts of Bangui, the Legion paratroopers watch...
(Yves Debay)

Right:
With the increase in firepower, and the excessive publicity given to all military losses, the French infantry at the end of this century wears armour and the Foreign Legion does not normally escape the rule, but in equatorial climates, wearing the 'Ninja' turtle equipment is not easy.
(Yves Debay)

Previous page:
The 4th company controlling movement in and out of the capital; the mission is to make sure that no weapons or ammunition get to the rebels, but also to keep the peace in order to get the local economy going again.
(Yves Debay)

Previous double page:
'The fish-men, the crocodile-men and the Mamie Watas [1] are going to come out of the river and devour the Frenchmen. The jujumen will throw bees up at the helicopters and they won't be able to fly any more!' The turbulent Yakomas' appeals to witchcraft did not stop the legionaries, here the 4th company from patrolling in the Bimbo quarter where calm had returned.
(Yves Debay)

———

4. Local version of the Lorelei, a witch or siren who lures men into the river

Left:
GCP watching over the dug-outs so that they can't be used to supply the rebels.
(Yves Debay)

Next page bottom right:
Occupying a brewery is often the best way in Africa of controlling a capital… it doesn't displease the legionaries either! Here the 4th company at the Mokaf Brewery. The colour of the beer crates is entirely fortuitous.
(Yves Debay)

Next page bottom right:
The M'baka population is not hostile to the presence of French soldiers, which is a godsend to the GCPs, like this NCO of Moroccan origin, always looking for information.
(Yves Debay)

Below:
With calm restored, training can start again, like this jump session over M'poko airport. marked by Homeric battles with the Godobe (little thieves) to stop them pinching the chutes.
(Yves Debay)

BRAZZA

OPERATION PELICAN

In spring 1997, Central Africa was again alight. Mobutu's Zaire was collapsing and the capture of Kinshasa by the troops of Laurent Désiré Kabila was expected at any time. To avoid panic and to carry out the evacuation of all the Europeans as calmly as possible, France put its troops into position early in Brazzaville, just on the other side of the Congo River which separates the two capitals. This was Operation *Pelican 1*. In the context, the 2e REP replaced the 8e RPIMa on 17 May 1997. It was Kinshasa that everybody was waiting for, when suddenly, instead, it was Brazzaville that was all ablaze. With a view to the forthcoming elections, the President, Pascal Lissouba, a Kongo, put out a decree that dissolved private militias. On 6 June, following on this decree, part of the regular army attacked the home of Sassou Nguesso, a Mbochis, a former president and leader of the 'Cobra' militia. The operation failed and set everything ablaze.

Part of the army went over to Sassou Nguesso whereas Lissouba had reinforcements come in from the provinces to support his 'Zulu' militiamen. Brazzaville was quickly cut in three, the south being controlled by a third militia, the 'Ninjas'. There was fighting with heavy weapons for control of the town centre.

The Congolese authorities were completely overtaken by events; the militiamen and soldiers were often drunk and drugged, and their officers had totally lost control of them. Several Europeans were molested.

Right:
This crossroads at the limit of the town and the industrial quarter was particularly dangerous as it was swept regularly by machine gun fire from a government 14.5 mm. Legionaries from the 1st company are here watching the spot to protect the ex-filtration of foreign
(Yves Debay)

Centre:
The legionaries can often do nothing but look on powerless at the sight of war. In the town centre a schoolboy has been killed by machine gun fire.
(Yves Debay)

Bottom right:
Legionaries carefully inspect a Mamba armoured vehicle of the Congolese army. A few days earlier, during an ambush, the legionaries returned fire and damaged a similar vehicle.
(Yves Debay)

Below:
In the devastated town, the VABs this one from the 1st company went out looking for foreign nationals cut off by the fighting between Cobras and Ninjas.
(Yves Debay)

BRAZZA

The REP therefore speeded up the evacuation of European nationals. In the night of 7 June, the 3rd platoon of the 1st company was violently attacked by Zulus not very far from the Presidency. An RPG-7 rocket seriously wounded three legionaries. Captain Trotignon, the commanding officer of the company succeeded in calming things down but the Congolese opened fire again on elements of the CEA and the ambulance which had come to evacuate the wounded. The radio operator of a GCP team was killed by a bullet to the heart.

This time the paratroopers reacted. A Mamba vehicle was hit by a grenade and 15 Zulus including one officer were killed. The Congolese fell back immediately and thereafter the REP was left well alone. These events made Paris decide to intervene. This became Operation *Pelican 2*. Reinforcements from the 8e RPIMa, the 2e REI and the 1er REC took over control of the airport whereas the REP and elements from the COS were entrusted with the evacuation operations. From the Orstom, a botanical research centre, where Colonel Puga

Right from top to bottom
These three shots show us men from the heavy mortar platoon who have borrowed some 4 X 4 vehicles lent by foreign nationals so that they can patrol in town. They are heavily armed: Minimi, RAC Apilas, FAMAS and rifle grenades stuffed into the pockets of the shrapnel-proof jackets.
(Yves Debay)

Below:
Leaving on a mission for these legionaries. Tension is high as this avenue is wide and goes from the airport to the town, offering wide open spaces, and is situated practically on the front line.
(Yves Debay)

75

BRAZZA

installed his command post, the 1st company, the CEA and the COS took part in the search for and the evacuation and safety of foreigners still present in Brazzaville.

Acting on information received from the embassy or from individuals, the Legion paratroopers formed up little convoys usually consisting of two VABs and a VBL (light Armored Car) in order to bring in the people who had been reported.

These missions were extremely dangerous because even though ever since the ' 7 June affair', French vehicles wereno longer directly targeted, there was heavy fighting and the Congolese would shoot at anything anywhere anyhow.

There was further proof that Africa had changed, all this shooting was not with old peashooters but with BM-21s and ZSU 23/4s and all the range of Soviet mortars. Often the regular army would start firing at the enemy just before the French convoy was to pass so as to attract the return fire on it. T he operation was over by 15 June at 18.00 and the French soldiers succeeded in evacuating 5 900 foreign nationals without loss.

The REP was the last to leave the country. A few hours before evacuating the Orstom, a salvo of four mortar shots riddled the chief of staff, Lieutenant-Colonel Morin's bags as well as the showers with shrapnel. Choosing to go and have a beer rather than washing himself probably saved the life of Lieutenant Perez-Pria, a Mexican serving in the 2e REP.

BOSNIA

In the summer of 1999, the 2e REP returned to Bosnia, the third time since its intervention at Sarajevo in 1993. In the context of the SFOR (Stabilisation Force) which had replaced the IFOR, it was on the outskirts of the Bosnian capital that the regiment's EMT was set up under the command of Lieutenant-Colonel Prévost. The unit was incorporated into the Franco-German centre of the Salamander Division. The Gebirgsjäger and the Legionaries got on well together.

More than once, the Legionaries' 'get up and go' surprised the German officers who were used to working with NATO conscripts. General Berger, the German commanding the brigade was delighted to be working with the Foreign Legion. For five months the REP patrolled a vast zone along the Montenegran border checking that the military part of the Dayton Agreements was being respected. The Legion parachutists of the 4th com-

pany and the CEA patrolled in wounded countryside, scarred by the war. The 2nd company was also in Bosnia at the same time but under French command with the brigade to the south of Mostar. At Raljovak, the EMT worked with the brigade in very multinational circumstances whilst the UCS, using CCL (Command and logistics commpany) staff and the 5th company, ensured support for the units in the field.

The regiment was deployed as a motorised force and the general calm enabled the command to launch a large-scale joint exercise with the Gebirgsjäger where VABs and FUCHS carried out a large number of armoured training raids. The only difference with a peace-time exercise, the presence of live ammunition in the vehicles and in the FAMAS magazines just in case…

Balkan reality caught up with the regiment at the end of its stay. Information reached SFOR HQ that the Croat and the Bosnian secret services,

Right:
The CEA has quit Milans and mortars to set up a check point in the Filipovichi region not far from the border with Montenegro. Zone control is part of the routine peace-keeping operations.
(Yves Debay)

Below:
The VBL of the captain commanding the 4th company has met a Luchs from the Aufklärung battalion seconded to the Franco-German Brigade. The Luchs platoon is under French command… an unusual situation for the Legion paratroopers.
(Yves Debay)

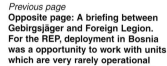

the HIS and the SNS were preparing 'anti-Dayton' action. Infiltration, spying, corrupting SFOR civil servants, threatening the PTI (international tribunal) at the Hagueand preparing attacks against diplomatic representatives. In order to counter these threats, the US General Ron Adams launched Operation Westar. Four official buildings, among which the HQ of the Mostar special police were taken over and searched. For this delicate operation, SFOR command used the REP. With speed, tact and precision, the legionaries took over the buildings at dawn on 14 October 1999.

Weapons, documents, counterfeiting equipment and 42 computers were taken. The only casualty was a policeman in civilian dress who tried to attack the legionaries with a metal bar and who was very quickly mastered. Several weeks later, the REP returned to Ballagne with the congratulations of all the SFOR.

Previous page
Opposite page: A briefing between Gebirgsjäger and Foreign Legion. For the REP, deployment in Bosnia was a opportunity to work with units which are very rarely operational in the same areas as the regiment.
(Yves Debay)

Right:
The 'Greys' invest an official building in Mostar, during Operation Westar.
(2e REP Sergent-chef Phillips)

KOSOVO

After undergoing intensive training at *La Courtine*, with the Gendamerie Mobile, the 1st company of the 2e REP went to Kosovo in April 2000. The mission was simple, designated CRO (Compagnie de Reserve Opérationelle - Operational Reserve Company) the company relieved the Marsouins of the 3e RIMa on the notorious Mitrovica Bridge.

This bridge across the River Ibar had become a symbol for the inhabitants of this divided town. In March the Marsouins guarded this passage and had to confront the thousands of Albanians who wanted to try force a passage which would have resulted in a blood-bath.

This was therefore a supervision mission, where necessary maintaining law and order. This was entrusted to the 1st company. The Legion paratroopers had to act with a lot of tact, knowing how not to react to provocation, to feel the increase in tension in a gathering crowd and then blocking the bridge when necessary. One of the problems that Captain X., commanding the company had, was finding the dividing line between keeping law and order and real fighting.

This was a complicated situation since in order to control the crowd, the men had to group together and block the thrusts of the demonstrators, thus giving a sniper a perfect target. Thus reaction drill and very careful instructions were given to the legionaries. They spent three months on the Mitrovica Bridge where their professionalism and coolness prevented many incidents from degenerating, particularly on 14 July when a rocket shot into the north of the town greatly increased tension in the town.

Another typical Kosovo mission was escorting Serbs who wanted to go to the Orthodox Church every Sunday. The church was in the Albanian sector and Sunday mass meant a large deployment of troops in Mitrovica.

In June 2000, the Legion paratroopers returned to Calvi having acquired a new skill —crowd control — a new capability for the regiment.

Below.
April 2000, on the Serbian side of the River Ibar. All is quiet: The REP takes care!
(Yves Debay)

Right:
**Polish armoured troops
in BMP-1s and legionaries protecting
orthodox worship at Mitrovica.
Perhaps an opportunity for
the black berets
of the Pomeranian division
to talk of home with
the green berets
of Polish origin.**
(Yves Debay)

Below:
**It is generally at night
that the tension mounts at Mitrovica.
Here the captain's two radio
operators are ready.**
(Yves Debay)

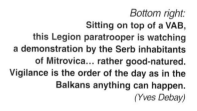

Bottom left
**When necessary, the legionaries
can put their 'keeping order' gear on.
The weight is noticeable as it includes
shrapnel-proof jackets, leggings,
arm protection, helmets and shields.**
(Yves Debay)

Bottom right:
**Sitting on top of a VAB,
this Legion paratrooper is watching
a demonstration by the Serb inhabitants
of Mitrovica… rather good-natured.
Vigilance is the order of the day as in the
Balkans anything can happen.**
(Yves Debay)

BOSNIA

The 2e REP found itself back in the ambiguous atmosphere of the Balkans again in January 2001, as a intervention reserve in the multinational brigade-north (MNB-North) of the KFOR under French command. The BIMOTO *(bataillon motorisé/mechanised battalion)* was made up of the CCL, the 3e and 4e Compagnies and the GCPs.

It is now almost two years since French troops were committed in Mitrovica where 450 legionaries arrived on 20 January under the command of Lieutenant-colonel Bouquin. The CCL, called UCL *(unité de commandement et logistique/logistics and command unit)* together with the CP settled into the 'trailer factory', an dirty old factory which had already been well set up by preceding units but which he 2e REP transformed as is the Foreign Legion's habit into a comfortable barracks. The two combat companies shared the BIMOTO's routine missions: being present in South Mitrovica, fighting trafficking, guarding roads and intelligence gathering.

All information arrived at the battalion's CP which sent them forward to the brigade for analysis. One of BIMOTO's missions was to protect the Serb enclave at Banja, which was totally isolated in the middle of Albanian villages. In order to watch the area, the legionaries set themselves up on the top a hill overlooking the village of Rutnik a real eagle's nest. In April, the UNMIK (UN mission in Kosovo) decided to tax commercial products entering Kosovo. For the Serbs, this decision was unacceptable because it meant a denial of their sovereignty and the de facto recognition of Kosovar independence. So they installed road blocks to impede the movements of the UNMIK inspectors. Operation Bélier had the legionaries force the barrages with the help of two MPGs *(Moyens polyvalents du Génie/miscellaneous engineering methods, i.e. multi-purpose vehicle)* and restore law and order.

The stay ended with another arms search operation in the Albanian sector which enabled a dozen automatic weapons to be recovered.

Patrolling in urban south Mitrovica.
(Yves Debay)

Top left:
Observation post near a Serb enclave.
(Yves Debay)

Top right:
**The night patrols allow them to combat
mafia-type activities and trafficking.**
(Yves Debay)`

Below:
**A mobile checkpoint, if it is set up very quickly
in the twenty minutes following a tip-off, the mobile
checkpoint can get results**
(Yves Debay)

THE 2e REP

TODAY

PERFECTLY ADAPTED TO CRISIS-SOLVING...

With the 2ᵉ REP, France has at its disposal a versatile fighting force which is perfectly adapted to crisis-solving. Because the Legion paratroopers are always available and because they can operate from the air, the 2ᵉ REP is considered as the 'first three days' regiment', as it can be sent thousands of miles from its bases. Nevertheless with the advent of mechanisation the regiment has evolved considerably, like the rest of the parachute forces in France.

Firepower has also increased greatly over the last few years even where it was least expected, like in Africa where guerrilla groups can afford to buy heavy equipment from ex-Warsaw pact arsenals. More than ever shooting kills and the 2ᵉ REP, like any other unit in the 11ᵉ parachute Brigade, has had to move with the times.

'We are still the 'three days' regiment', but we can last longer because the VABs will arrive within 48 hours after an OAP (Opération Aéroportée - Airborne Operation) and enable us to continue the operation; this does not prevent us being recovered to do another operation from the air. All the richness of the REP in the Year 2000 is being both Paratrooper and mechanised', said the Corps Commander, Colonel Prévost.

This transformation has created other logistics problems which have been solved by creating the 5th company, the only repairs and maintenance company to exist within a parachute regiment. This is an extra advantage in a regiment which already has a lot.

Another deployment method which is likely to evolve, since the 11ᵉ Parachute Brigade has taken over missions formerly given over to the 1ᵉʳ Regiment d'Infanterie *(1st InfantryRegiment)*: the use of helicopters.

This of course is nothing new in the REP since the REP carries out one or two ALAT exercises every year and often works with the Navy's Frelon helicopters.

The companies' specialising also contributes to the regiment's strength; thus, for a long time, the 2ᵉ company was the only professional mountain infantry combat unit within the Armée de Terre (the French Army).

During Operation *Almandin* (Chad), two combat companies, if the general commanding the French troops so wished, could have lined up some forty sharpshooters, an exceptional strike force, particularly well-adapted to the operations of that type of theatre.

In 2001, the 2e REP means 1 297 young, athletic, resistant legionaries, among which there are 1 000 assault troops who have a high level of equipment and efficiency.

The majority of legionaries are officer material and many of them are commando monitor level.

The Legion paratroopers come from 60-odd countries, about a third speak French, the rest do not. As the Foreign Legion is often involved in world events, recruitment from Eastern block countries is on the up.

The average age is 24 and all the officers take pleasure in saying that the modern legionary has the same qualities as his elders.

The reasons for joining are varied: the taste for adventure, the desire to escape from a monotonous pre-determined existence, the wish to break with the past or simply the search for a higher quality of life.

But what differentiates a legionary from any other soldier in any army, is that when he joins, he already has a whole lot of experience of life. The decision to join up always stems from this experience, be it happy or unhappy, and this brings the regiment a certain maturity and serenity which few units can claim to have. In a military context, this is practically unique because each legionary is conscious that he has taken a decision which can take him to the extremes of what can humanly be asked of someone, and he is prepared to go that far!

Below:
Be they young legionaries of GCPs, war-hardened and very specialised, all the members of the 2e REP share the same ideals and the same faith in the regiment. Here members of the GCP are carrying out hostage rescue training in urban surroundings.
(Yves Debay)

Above:
Like the rest of the Foreign Legion, the 2ᵉ REP likes to improve its living space. CEA artists have here decorated a door of the Fillipovici post in Bosnia in their own way.
(Yves Debay)

The reader will no doubt be surprised to find these two pages about the spirit of the Legion paratrooper in this part of the book given over to the operational capacities of the regiment.

A unique shock unit

The explanation is simple: the 2ᵉ REP only exists because each man from the simple legionary to the Corps Commander, has been imbued with the spirit so characteristic of the Legion Paratrooper. When this type of soldier was created in 1946, a lot of people betted on the unit disappearing rapidly, putting forward the idea that the versatility of the paratrooper and the heaviness of the Foreign Legion were incompatible… and yet the BEP and the REP have earned their place on the paths to glory; nowadays, thanks to this rather special spirit the 2ᵉ REP is France's unique shock unit.

One cannot explain a spirit; it lives daily in the regiment. It is difficult in a few pages to describe to the uninitiated what inspires each member of this prestigious regiment. The first thing which strikes the observer who is lucky enough to frequent the unit, is the total commitment of each of its members.

No half measures here; the rigour of the 'Old Legion' is ever-present in daily life, even in apparently insignificant tasks. The simple fact that they would present themselves in a regulation and

legionary manner took the officers of the German Gebirgsjäger, who recently shared the REP's activities in Bosnia, totally by surprise. Attention to detail was so strong as to irritate other soldiers working with the REP. A Legion paratrooper is a Legion Paratrooper 24 hours a day, and those who cannot keep up the rhythm, particularly the officers, do not remain in the regiment for long.

This natural selection process does mean however that the corps' command cells are homogeneous; everybody has known everybody for years. There's little familiarity between officers and soldiers - the Legion system would not allow it - but there is certainly collusion between them.

Considered as one big family

The 2ᵉ REP can be considered as one big family. But to get in, the start is particularly difficult, especially in the lower ranks. It is not at all easy to be young second-lieutenant in the REP, to such an extent that other units criticise the ways in which the Legion paratroopers are formed, but once this manner of command and way of life have been mastered, the young officer has every chance of becoming a 'Repman' for the remainder of his career.

'The more rigorous you are, the less stressed you are', as Colonel Puga liked to say.

This rigour in daily life does not prevent them from enjoying life and the 2ᵉ REP is hardly a sad regi-

Below:
The 2ᵉ REP in the 1998 14 July march-past.
(Yves Debay)

ment. Whistling and singing are often to be heard in the corridors, proof of the unit's young character. This youth of character is also due to intensive sporting activities which keep thethe legionaries in excellent physical condition.

Some have compared this almost entirely male community with a congregation of soldier monks. Soldiers, certainly; monks certainly not since rigour in the execution of daily chores does not prevent them from having fun as the atmosphere of the streets in Calvi at night or during the Fête des Rois amply demonstrates.

Often having no home, the legionary considers that all the world is his home and everywhere he goes, he always sets himself very comfortably, working hard to clear and embellish the site. The messes are warm places which are to be found in all four corners of the planet. When they leave, every thing is clean, like in Brazzaville where, in a town given over to looting, the REP did not leave a single dirty paper in the billets it had occupied. This last cleaning up chore being carried out practically under fire.

The REP is also 'Grande Légion' with its cult of tradition and the Camerone Day celebrations which glorify the Unit and the sacred duty of carrying out the mission to the end… a permanent state of mind in the REP.

Above:
Care brought to each detail is part and parcel of REP life, here during a simple learning session. This Training Sergeant does the equipment check before the jump for his students.
(Yves Debay)

Left:
The lieutenant commanding the 1st platoon of the 4th company discovers German combat rations with his men during a frugal meal in a Bosnia post. Sharing daily life helps to join officers and legionaries in the spirit of the regiment.
(Yves Debay)

Below:
Be it on manœuvres in he field or during th most dangerous exercises, the men in the 1st platoon learn the meaning of the REP spirit sometimes painfully, always after a lot of effort.
(Yves Debay)

ORGANISATION

Headquarters

Logistic and Command Company

1st Combat Company

5th Company (Mechanics and support)

2nd Combat Company

Reconnaissance and Support Company

3rd Combat Company

Base and Training Company

4th Combat Company

The 'first three days' regiment...

With the 1er RCP, the 3e and 8e RPI-Ma, the 2e REP is a parachute infantry regiment which belongs to the 11e Parachute Brigade.

In the last two decades, many have bet on the disappearance of the parachute infantry arm, in their opinion too light to stand the shock of modern warfare, but events have proved them wrong, that the airborne soldier is not finished and still very useful thanks to his versatility.

The efficiency and the lightness of modern anti-tank weapons together with strategic and tactical suppleness could enable any TAP unit to reach the 'three days' fight' zone and even face a conventional enemy.

The organisation of the regiment is that of a standard TAP regiment,

— with headquarters,

— four combat companies,

— one logistics and command company (CCL),

— one reconnaissance and support company (CEA)

— and the very new base and training company (CBI).

— To this must be added, and this is special to the 2e REP, the 5th company, which is a support unit.

Each combat company has a command platoon, three combat platoons and one support platoon. The companies are above all lightly equipped parachute infantry companies; but the length of the legionary's contract and operational needs have enabled the companies to specialise.

The merit for this goes to Colonel Caillaud, who just after the war in Algeria, understood the usefulness of specialisation in the context of modern warfare. Combat companies have specialised as follows:

— **1st:** originally night and anti-tank fighting, now urban warfare.

— **2nd:** mountain fighting.

— **3rd:** amphibious operations.

— **4th:** destruction and sniping.

Less shut away than the other units in the 11e BP (Parachute Brigade) based in South West France, the 2e REP has found an ideal training ground at Balagne, where its companies can take advantage of the terrain, the sea and climate, ideal for military parachute jumps.

The 2e REP is above all 120 crack troops serving the Republic like these young Legion paratroopers in the 4th company perched on a Lohr (Mule)
(Yves Debay)

THE LEGION PARATROOPER

There were officially 963 Legion paratroopers in 1999. Serving in the 2e REP is a dream for many youngsters.

At 18, the myth of the Legion paratrooper is real, but the road there is long and only the best will be awarded the fourragère in the colours of the Légion d'Honneur. The adventure begins at Aubagne where the first selection is carried out by psycho-physical means and security enquiries to eliminate all mythomaniacs, delinquants [1] and those who cannot live in a group. Then it is in the 4e RE, the Legion's training regiment, based at Castelnaudary, that the young candidate learns the basics of his new trade. From the first week, he can ask to join the 2e REP. But to do so, he will have to be at the head of his section by sheer willpower. Youth, total availability, rigour, strength of character, a taste for adventure and especially perfect physical condition are all the qualities which are expected of the future Legion paratrooper.

At the end of four months' training, the best arrive at Calvi. He who thinks that he has finished train-

ing, discovers that he still has everything to learn. The 'year' he is in will enable him to obtain the famous paratrooper wings in three weeks with six jumps. Finally, the red fourragère is awarded during a short and moving ceremony on the sacred Raffali Way. The Elders, in combat companies, are present to welcome the new Legion paratrooper.

Life for a legionary with the 2e REP can be described as a succession of periods spent at Calvi, interrupted by manoeuvres, periods 'revolving' abroad, operations and courses to complete his training.

During his first year, after getting his paratrooper wings, the young legionary joins one of the combat companies where he is endlessly 'brought up to standard'. Some of them are lucky enough to take part in a real operation as soon as they arrive, like the chap from the Vosges in the 1st company wounded in the ambush in Brazzaville on 6 June 1999.

---

1. *Unlike what is normally supposed, the Foreign Legion does not accept criminals.*

Bottom:
The legionary's condition is to be constantly challenging himself. Here a rope crossing exercise in the citadel at Calvi.
(Yves Debay)

Next page:
Portrait of an AA-52 server in Bosnia during the REP second stay. The average age of the Legion paratroopers is 23.
(Yves Debay)

During his second year's service and according to his capacities and service record, the legionary will be directed along one of the following channels.

F1: Promotion to the rank of sergeant before the end of the first contract.

F2: promotion to the rank of sergeant before the end of seven year's service.

F3: Promotion to the rank of corporal after six year's service.

Once a year, the legionary has an interview with the Corps Commander, who will personally direct him. The legionaries are also encouraged in their career to serve two years abroad in the 13e DBLE in Djibouti, with the 3e REI in Guyana or with the DLEM at Mayotte.

NATIONALITIES IN THE 2ᵉ REP

There is a rather impressive variety of nationalities in the 2ᵉ REP.

The parachutists come from all over the planet, as is shown by this list drawn up in 2001.

First of all 250 Frenchmen.

Western Europe has 12 Germans, 1 Austrian, 10 Belgians, 44 Englishmen, 1 Scot, 16 Spaniards, 10 Irishmen, 12 Italians, 14 Luxemburgers, 9 Monacans, 1 Dutchman, 30 Portuguese and 65 Swiss.

Nothern Europe has 4 Danes, 10 Finns, 1 Icelander, 1 Norwegian and 5 Swedes.

On the other side of the Atlantic: 4 Americans 60 Canadians, 3 Mexicans for the North

(All photographs by Yves Debay)

and 1 Argentinean, 5 Brazilians, 1 Chilean, 1 Peruvian, 1 Uruguayan for the South.

There are 2 Australians and 5 New-Zealanders.

From the Far East, there are 1 Chinese, 12 Koreans, 13 Japanese, 1 Laotian and 1 Nepalese. There are 3 Kazakhs, 1 Kirghiz and 3 Uzbeks from Central Asia.

The Middle East is the least reresented regions with 3 Lebanese and 4 Turks. North

Africa with 2 Algerians, 7 Moroccans and 2 Tunisians does not provide many men. The rest of Africa supplies 1 man from Bénin, 1 Ethiopian, 8 Malgaches and 3 South-Aficans.

Central and Eastern Europe, after Western Europe, has the lion's share with 3 Albanians, 18 Belorussians, 11 Bulgarians, l0 Croats, 3 Estonians, 68 Hungarians, 10 Latvians, 19 Lithuanians, 4 Moldavians, 115 Poles, 55 Romanians, 55 Russians, 46 Slovaks, 2 Slovenes, 39 Czechs and 49 Ukrainians.

Numbering 250, they are the wealth of the regiment, from which they are drawn thanks to their experience and pride in their situation. With their president, normally a *major* (roughly equivalent to Staff Sergeant Major) they are also the regiment's memory. The average age is 34 and unendingly the NCOs of the 2e REP constantly challenging themselves by attending courses with the 4e RE, at the Pau ETAP *(Ecole des troupes parachutistes/Airborne troop school)*, at the Mont-Louis CNEC (Centre national D'entrainement commando/National commando training center), at the infantry application school, at the Chamonix EMHM *(Ecole militaire de haute montagne/Alpine Military School)* and in different Army technical institutes.

The living strength of the REP, they are men like that huge Turkish Staff-Sergeant in the CEA, Milan specialist and leader of men, that Spanish Staff-Sergeant who knows how to speak to dogs and who commands the dog platoon, that Moroccan Warrant-Officer from the GCP specialised in beacons or that other staff-Sergeant always in a good mood and who, far from the fury of the fight takes over the CP secretariat.

As in all western armies, in the 2e REP, the NCOs are the lifeline between command and the legionaries who have come from so many different places. This presupposes that apart from having the necessary natural authority, they must have good experience of human nature.

In the REP as in the rest of the Legion, the NCOs are constantly listening to their men whilst demanding total commitment from them in their daily task of being a soldier.

Good humour and modesty rule supreme in the NCOs' mess; those who drink at the trophy-lined bar have a high opinion of their regiment and not themselves.

Previous page top:
This young sergeant is leading his men, during a helicopter operation at Calvi. He shows both the dynamism of the regiment and that of the NCOs.
(Yves Debay)

Previous page bottom:
On an obstacle course, an NCO from the 1ᵉ company leads his men.
(Yves Debay)

Right:
A staff-sergeant in the 4ᵗʰ company carrying the 4ᵗʰ company's pennant. Note the black képi for the officers, the fourragère of the Légion d'Honneur, the regimental insignia and a very nice series of flashes, showing hat this NCO has taken part in a lot of overseas operations.
(Yves Debay)

HONNEUR

63 officers serve in the 2e REP, from the officer cadet to the Corps Commander, from the second-lieutenant to the major, all have the feeling of belonging to a prestigious community. Some have come up through the ranks, like this Yugoslav captain, a former president of the NCOs who has become company commander.

The Corps Commander leads the regiment and according to his personality imposes his own brand and ways of doing things.

Only very outstanding officers can expect to command the REP and some of them have marked contemporary military history like Lieutenant-Colonel Jean Pierre, killed in Algeria or Lieutenant-Colonel Erulin who jumped at the head of the regiment over Kolwezi.

Perhaps more than anywhere else, in the REP, the regiment forms one body with its 'Boss' and the Corps Commander's style shows through in the way the officers and legionaries go about their business.

The senior officers, including the Corps Commander, 5 lieutenant-colonels and two majors. Almost all of them have made the Legion their career. Their rank does not prescribe taking part in high level sporting activities, like this second-in-command, test parachutist and veteran diver and jumper.

Generally, the captains are young 'lords', mellowed by responsibility. Commanding an REP company is a privilege envied throughout all the infantry but which demands exceptional qualifications. The essential substance of airborne combat and the variety of operational theatres where the REP functions can mean a company being completely cut off; in this case, the captain is master of his fate and that of his men.

With the 2e REP, a lieutenant has to hang in there, and for fresh young officer, just out from St-Cyr, a transfer to the regiment is an honour but also an apprenticeship among the hardest of the hard. Many corps commanders and even some high-level personalities in the French Army began their career as a lieutenant with the Legion Paratroopers.

Efficiency does not mean a lack of imagination and good humour as is proved by the incessant activity of that lieutenant of Mexican origin who came up through the ranks, capable of running a combat command post and unearthing a case of Château Margaux in raging Brazzaville.

Top:
The 'Soleil ' (sun) pennant traditionally the radio sign of the Corps Commander seen here on the antenna of a P-4 during Operation Pelican in Brazzaville.
(Yves Debay)

Left:
This lieutenant of the 2nd company has been photographed in action at the CEITO. In the 2e REP, the young officers have to give their best in order to impress their senior officers, and their legionaries who often have many years' more experience.
(Yves Debay)

Next page:
During a tactical exercise in Corsica, two captains with their faces camouflaged, study the map.
(Yves Debay)

THE THIRD DIMENSION

The modern conflicts in the Gulf and Balkan areas, seem to have relegated the paratrooper - a light and unprotected soldier - to a second-class role. Faced with the challenges posed by professionalisation and the new policies of the country, the Armée de Terre (the French Army), might be tempted to cut its airborne capabilities considerably.

'What use are paratroopers who cost so much to train now that we are less and less involved with our former colonies and now that any old regiment can supply companies for a 'revolving' mission?'

The answer lies in the multitude of potential new threats which the new century will throw up for us. The two opposing Cold War blocks have disappeared but more than ever Old Europe is dependent for energy sources and raw materials. Keeping the oil-producing countries within the western sphere of influence and keeping control of the supply routes will no doubt be one of the big challenges of the 21st century. This type of conflict has already begun in Central Asia with the localised fighting for the control of the pipelines. Tomorrow, things like Central Africa and the fabulous oil reserves in the Gulf of Guinea will no doubt be at stake. In this domain

France and therefore Europe have retained their historical and cultural importance. If our allies are aggressed, France must react and win the battle of the *'three first days'*. To reinforce the increasingly skeleton units or to intervene as quickly as possible to help allied governments, it is imperative to be able to drop or air-transport paratroopers. With the 11e Parachute Brigade, France remains one of the only countries to have qualified, war-hardened paratroopers who already know the terrain. This remarkable tool which includes the 2e REP must be preserved, even if it means being europeanised with the setting up of an airborne rapid reaction force equipped with heavy FLA transport aircraft. The rapid pre-positioning of a part of the regiment at Dakar on Christmas night 1999, following the coup d'état in Ivory Coast proves how well the 2e REP is able to operate in the *'3rd dimension'*. This 'airborne' know-how is maintained at a high level of competence thanks to frequent jumping sessions either on manoeuvres or over the two DZs (drop zones) the regiment has in Corsica

THE ABILITY OF THE REP TO OPERATE IN THE 'THIRD DIMENSION'

If it is called upon to operate in its parachute capacity for immediate action, the 2e REP can supply the equivalent of a GAP (Groupement Aéroportée - airborne group) including headquarters, two combat and one support companies.

Deployment is of course carried out in relation to the distance, the strategic and tactical conditions, and the Air Force's transport capability. The 440 men of a GAP can be parachuted, by a tactical group of eight to ten planes.

It is already known that French forces are handicapped when planning strategic operations by the lack of long-range heavy transport planes. While waiting for the FAP *(Force aérienne de Projection/Airborne projection force)* crews' worth to be recognised, the Air Force continues to ensure its transport functions for the deployment and the training of the parachute regiments with C-160 Transall and C-130 Hercules aircraft.

The airborne capability of the 2e REP is permanently ensured by the proximity of Sainte-Catherine airport at Calvi; the 2e REP has the use of one aircraft twice a month to carry out its training jump sessions. Depending on the weather forecasts, drops are carried out over the regiment's DZ which is near the Raffalli quarter or at Borgo, on the other side of the island. The regiment does 13 000 jumps every year.

The future legionaries are trained and receive their wings within the regiment and not at the ETAP at Pau (see the Chapter on CBI) which is unique in the *Armée* (land forces)

Above: **CEA men have just received their parachutes and are equipped.**
(Yves Debay)

Below:
Ten years after Kolwezi, operational atmosphere on the tarmac at Toulouse-Francasal… The REP is getting ready to jump during the *Frégate 98* manoeuvres whose aim was the rescuing of foreign nationals. This airborne know-how is kept at a high level through constant *(Yves Debay)*

ORDERING...

Left: **Forming the sticks for a training jump. Some parachutists are jumping without equipment harness whereas others are jumping with full combat gear and equipment.**
(Yves Debay)

Below right:
Typical of the REP, the coloured triangle on the helmet enables quick mustering after the jump.
(Yves Debay)

Bottom:
As dawn breaks, an adjudant-chef inspects his men.
(Yves Debay)

It is the TAP officer, usually a captain who is in charge of the regiment's jump sessions. In liaison with the SAER *(Service Aérien du Regiment/Regimental air service)*, the first office job is to order the aircraft, make out a jump order and allocate the places.

The companies are then told when to present themselves at the airfield depending on the weather forecast and the availability of Air Force planes.

The parachutes are stored with the regiment are handed out on the tarmac generally at Sainte-Catherine, at Calvi.

CHECKING...

Then, what is called *'avionage'* in paratrooper jargon, comes next; this enables the platoons to be allocated their places inside their respective aircraft. In a well-established order, the completely equipped men are lined up and the sticks are constituted. A stick is a group of soldiers who will jump at the signal of the jump-master.

A Transall can carry 56 fully-equipped troops. In combat the plane can only make one fly-over and must drop all its paratroopers in one go, but during manoeuvres or a training jump, the sticks can be parachuted in several passes.

Everybody has to know his place and the order in which he has to jump.

Each paratrooper is then checked. The jump-masters and sometimes the platoon heads go through the ranks and check the equipment very carefully.

The slightest mistake has the direst consequences. Then they have to wait for a more or less long time and this wait is all the more difficult because of the weight of the parachutes and the straps which hinder all movement.

Above:
In the correct order the sticks move off awkwardly because of the weight of all the equipment to board the aircraft.
(Yves Debay)

ABOARD...

The parachutists sit on four canvas benches along the length of the aircraft. The trip is often not very pleasant because of the heat, the noise, the length of the flight and the cumbersome equipment which hinders all movement.

Ten minutes from the DZ, the jump-master gives the command ' Get up, hook up' and a red light comes on. The men fold back the benches and hook the SOA *(Sangle d'Ouverture Automatique/automatic opening line)* snap clasp on to the cable that runs the length of the fuselage. The jump-master walks past the stick and checks everything one last time. The hold door is opened and the slipstream engulfs the cabin. A horn sounding, the light turning green and the *'go!'* from the jump-master are the jump signals.

With one hand on the ventral strap, the men throw themselves into space. 1, 2, 3, a pull and the parachute opens.

They have to check that it has opened properly, if not they have to open the emergency chute. In the air, the paratroopers are very vulnerable, but the height from which they drop rarely exceeds 200 m in war-time, and does not give them time to admire the countryside. Moreover sometimes they have to pull on the ropes so as not fall down into the others and so as to locate the DZ.

They land 'nose to the wind'. A few seconds before landing, the paratroopers have to get rid of their harness... then the shock of landing can be very brutal indeed.

Above:
In the correct order the sticks move off awkwardly because of the weight of all the equipment to board the aircraft.
(Yves Debay)

Left:
'Stand up! Hook up!' In a few moments these men will be out in empty space.
(Sergent-chef Phillips - 2e REP)

Below:
dropping from a Transall which, with the C-130, is the main transport plane in the Air Force.
(Yves Debay)

RE-GROUPING...

The most difficult part of any drop as all the great airborne operations in history — Crete, Normandy or Arnhem — have shown, is mustering all the troops once they have landed. A fighting unit then has to be made up from the mass of soldiers lost in the night and scattered by the wind. The majority of operational drops are made during the night. As soon as he reaches the ground, the paratrooper roughly folds his chute, takes his weapon out of its sheath and starts to look for the assembly point designated for the briefing. On the way, he picks up his mates. Re-grouping can be made easier by whistles, and by day, pennants with the company colours, etc... The coloured triangles at the back of the helmets make identification and re-grouping easier. Once assembled and radio links established, the company tries to set up a security perimeter to protect the drop zone and make the landing easier for the following waves of paratroopers and heavy equipment.

TRANSPORT BY HELICOPTER AND ASSAULT LANDING

Above:
**Legion paratroopers from
the 4th company, practising loading
and unloading procedures during
an ALAT campaign in Calvi.**
(Yves Debay)

Next page top right:
**During the *Frégate 98* exercise, legio-
naries practice an assault landing.
Here a section spills from the rear of
a Transall to 'occupy' Rodez airport.**
(Yves Debay)

Next page center:
**The 2e company being transported
by helicopter over Borgo. With the
help of Pumas from the RAF during
the *Winged Crusader 95* exercise
where Legion paratroopers
co-operated with the 'Red Devils',
the famous English paratroopers**
(Yves Debay

In the context of the 'third dimension' and of its normal light infantry mission operating from aircraft, the 2e REP has also mastered the techniques of air transport and helicopter transport.

Air transport consists of deploying a combat unit, generally a company, by means of aircraft which will carry out an assault landing. This method is particularly suitable to Africa. The Israeli paratrooper raid on Entebbe is still the archetype for this type of operation.

On a landing zone, secured or not (in the first case, the GCP group of the division which includes the REP's GCP will have taken control of the airport), one or more transport aircraft land, come to rest as quickly as possible with engines still running and unload soldiers and vehicles from the rear ramp before taking off again. The operation lasts five minutes at most. This type of very risky operation is only used if the weather forecast is unsuitable for an OAP or for a rapid strike operation of the *'seize and hold'* type for which the troops must not be dispersed.

In the Armée 2000 plan, the bulk of helicopter-borne operations which were carried out by the 1er RI, will now be carried out by the 11th Parachute Brigade. For the paratroopers, working from helicopters is of course nothing new because since the Algerian war, Red and Green Berets have always used helicopters and are even at the origin of this method.

The 2e REP has kept and improved this 'science' learnt by the great veterans. Two or three times a year, the ALAT dispatches one of its flights to Calvi so that the Legion paratroopers can practice helicopter-borne combat. The proximity of the Naval Air base at St Mandrier enables the Navy's Super Frelon helicopters to be used in Corsica.

Next page bottom:
**The Marine Nationale also takes part in airborne exercises
with the 11e BP. Here a Super Frelon
has just dropped men from the 4th company.**
(Yves Debay)

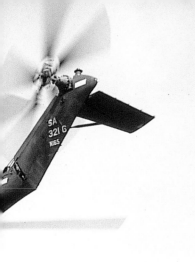

MECHANISED COMBAT

Right:
Legion paratroopers spill out from a VAB. For many of the legionaries who have come from the Eastern Block, mechanised combat is nothing new.
(Yves Debay)

Next page:
It is in the daily training sessions that the gestures and movements are learned which, in battle, will make all the difference. Here a briefing session before a mechanised exercise.
(Yves Debay)

Next page bottom:
A column of VABs seen at la Courtine where the 2e REP is training for deployment in the Balkans.
(Sergent-chef Phillips - 2ᵉ REP)

Below:
In Brazzaville, during Operation *Pélican*, the VAB was used as an armoured bus to evacuate foreign nationals. Here the Legion paratroopers are going to escort a group from a catholic school.
(Yves Debay)

Armoured Legion Paratroopers! The mind of many a Green Beret boggled at this new way of fighting which might have meant the end of the supple, feline and manoeuvring paratrooper. Back in 1946, turning heavy legionaries into paratroopers had also been severely criticised… and yet the idea caught on and finished by giving France one of its best regiments.

Mechanisation is but the result of the natural evolution of conflicts which began in the sixties. This evolution was evidenced by a large increase in firepower especially in the operational theatres where the parachute division had to operate. Moreover, the flaring up of the situation in the Balkans, implicated the REP in peace-keeping missions where the regiment lost all its mobility and placed itself between the belligerents, thereby risking getting caught in the crossfire without any possibility of manoeuvring. Thankless, unpopular missions but ones in which it was nice to be able to count on a bit of armour. In 1992, in Sarajevo, the REP learnt to appreciate one of its future combat tools… and the triangular decal was soon stuck on to the glacis of the white UN VABs

It has now got into the habit, but at the begining the regiment had to adopt the 'armoured' spirit with-

out losing its paratrooper's soul. The three last Corps Commanders have made sure of that. For the simple legionary, this is not really a problem because many of them, and particularly those from the Eastern Block have had experience of armoured combat in their respective countries.

The officers have learnt to operate 'under armour' and quickly appreciated the advantage offered by an armoured vehicle. Thanks to the VAB, the regiment can in fact remain for a longer period on the ground without losing its paratrooper spirit. The 2e REP used VABs in operations in Bosnia, Kosovo, and during the evacuation under fire of nationals from Brazzaville.

As proof of the importance that the General Staff attached to the VAB during the latest deployment in Bosnia, the 4th company and the CEA carried out motorised manoeuvres, including stopping, recovery, reconnaissance and outflanking just as any other mechanised regiment in Cold War Germany.

The 2e REP has got 74 VABs, divided among the combat companies, 12 per company.

THE PARACHUTE INFANTRY

The Legion Paratrooper is above all a shock soldier. Even if he is specialised, the Green Beret's primary mission is infantry fighting. His training and his team spirit has readied him for the fray. The four combat companies are the regiment's fer-de-lance and can be used for airborne operations, motorised fighting with VABs or in helicopter-borne operations.

Twentieth century operations can very well lead a company to carry out law enforcement operations, like the 1st company which went on a course with the Gendarmerie with a view to being sent to Kosovo in the spring of 2000. The combat company has 130 men at its disposal divided into three combat and one support platoons.

These platoons are commanded by a lieutenant or an NCO, a warrant-officer or a staff-sergeant. The platoon is itself divided into three combat and one support sections. The combat section commanded by a sergeant has 10 men, and consists of a Minimi light machine gun, a sniper equipped with an FR-F2, an LRAC anti-tank rocket launcher and gunner, a LGI rocket launcher and operator and two voltigeurs (infantryman). Depending on the type of mission, the section can have three types of close-quarters anti-tank weapon, the 89 mm LRAC, its successor the AT-4 or the RAC APILAS, a 112 mm rocket launcher which is not necessarily very easy to handle but which does have destructive power.

The support section at platoon level has two Eryx launchers. This pocket missile launcher can be fired like the AT-4 from within a closed area; its powerful hollow-charge warhead is able to destroy any modern combat tank up to a distance of 600m.

The captain also has a support section equipped with two Milan launchers. This section also includes a group with a VAB equipped with a 20 mm canon in which there is also a HECATE PGM launcher. The combination of these two weapons allows for precision long-distance shots or for shooting back effectively at enemy snipers. During these missions, the company commander can also count on a very reliable weapon, the good old Browning.50 machine gun used atop the VABs or on a tripod during airborne operations.

The company's organisation is often 'disturbed' and adapted to the mission in hand. The Eryxes and MILANs can all be regrouped together if there is a persistent armour threat. The weapons carried will depend on whether the regiment uses VABs or is airlifted. French infantry firepower has thus developed considerably in delivery effectiveness and mastery of weapons systems; the 2e REP remains an unrivalled combat force.

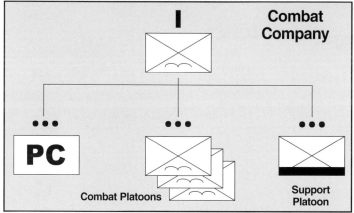

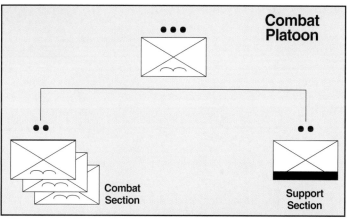

Top:
The combat section.
(Yves Debay)

Right:
**Designating a target at the CEITO.
From this photo can be seen
how infantry fighting
is the work of a team**
(Yves Debay)

Previous page:
**An LRAC operator with his server
leaping forward during an exercise
in the camp at Larzac.
Note the rockets hanging
from the back
of the TAP backpack.**
(Yves Debay)

INFANTRY WEAPONS

ASSAULT RIFLE *FAMAS*

When it entered service, at the beginning of the eighties, this revolutionary assault rifle was called a little derisively the 'Clairon' (Bugle). Since then it has proved its effectiveness, by its precision, compactness, ease of maintenance. It is the legionaries' everyday companion and he must look after it as he would do a mistress.

Inset right:
In Brazzaville during *Pélican 2*, a legionary in the 1e company is watching the fighting. An attacker would not stand a chance against his laser-sighted Famas, if the order was given to fire.
(Yves Debay)

Right: **Tens of thousands of cartridges are fired off every year in training sessions on the rifle ranges south of Calvi. Everyone's skill in shooting is taken into account.**
(Yves Debay)

Below: **Perfect firing position for this legionary in the 2[e] company who is leaning his Famas on his TAP bag.**
(Yves Debay)

RIFFLE GRENADE

The Foreign Legion has always favoured this weapon fired from the Famas rifle. Well-aimed and used in salvoes, this weapon is deadly, but using it needs intensive training... which of course is the case for the REP. Three types of grenades can be used.

Firing session, with the anti-personnel rifle grenade, in the Central African Republic during one of the 4th company's tours of duty.
(Yves Debay)

PRECISION RIFLE
FR-F2

This precision rifle has replaced the FR-F1. The French Army's doctrine on how to use infantry has always favoured the use of sharp-shooters in the group, even before the modern fashion for sniping prevalent in today's armies. In Kolwezi, where they were sometimes grouped together, the sharpshooters worked wonders against the African fighters unused to this type of fighting.

Right.
In Brazzaville, this FR-F2 server in the 1st company perched on a VAB is ready to respond to any attack. In Africa, this type of shooting is most dissuasive.

Below:
Other conflicts, other tactics. In the Balkans, sharpshooting is one of the most frequently used combat methods. It is only for the photograph that you can see the rifle and the face of the sniper. Otherwise at less than ten metres, nothing can be seen at all.
(Yves Debay)

LIGHT MACHINE GUN MINIMI

This light machine gun is what the French Infantry needed. Light, compact and robust, the Minimi gives tremendous firepower to the assault groups because its features and its handling enable the legionaries to attack with it

The 4th company was one of the first companies in the French army to be given the Minimi, in order to evaluate it.
(Yves Debay)

LIGHT MACHINE GUN AA-52

Going back to the Algerian war, the light machine gun AA-52 is still in service. Although a weapon from another generation, it is still reliable and the REP still uses it, particularly as a sort of Bren gun, with a bipod.

This heavily-laden legionary, armed with the bipod version of the AA-52 getting ready for an assault landing.
(Yves Debay)

Its size and its rate of fire make the Minimi an ideal weapon for urban fighting, seen here being used at Hammelburg by the 1st company.

MACHINE GUN BROWNING M-2 CAL.50

Indispensable and indestructible, the Browning M-2 Cal 50, known by the name '12.7' in the French army will easily last into the next century. Its is mounted on the VABs, but also on a tripod, supporting the company.

Hunched over his 12.7, this server in the 2nd company is firing for all he's worth in spite of the NBC alert.

AT ROCKET LAUNCHER
LRAC 89 mm

Powerful and simple to use, the 89 mm Lance-Roquette Anti-Char (*Anti-tank rocket launcher)* is the French infantry's classic anti-tank weapon.

**LRAC server
in the 2ⁿᵈ company
at the CEITO.**

LIGHT ROCKET
LAUNCHER *AT-4*

Of Swedish origin, this disposable light rocket launcher has appearedin the French army. Although it may not destroy a tank it can damage it; it is, however used against light armour or entrenched positions.

**This legionary in the 4ᵉ, who
is about to fire his
AT-4 on the firing range
at Larzac is waiting
for the order to fire.**

LIGHT MISSILE
LAUNCHER *ERYX*

This is truly a pocket missile. It can be fired in an enclosed area and has enormous destructive power thanks to its warhead which can destroy any modern tank.

**Firing the ERYX
is quite spectacular.
An instructor from
the 4ᵗʰ helps a young server
from the 2ⁿᵈ at Larzac.**

THE CEITO

Like all the other French Army infantry companies, the companies from the 2ᵉ REP are tested once a year at the CEITO (Centre d'Entraînement et d'Instruction aux Tirs Operationnels -The Operational Firing Training and Instruction Centre) at the camp at Larzac. After two weeks training in the regiment the company goes with all its normal equipment to the CEITO. At the end of a week's reconnaissance and after a first evaluation, the company has to carry out a series of tactical firing exercises over a defined course. The first phase is offensive, the second defensive and the third consists of holding a position during a night attack. Along with the FAMAS which each Legion paratrooper carries, all the support weapons, Minimi, AA-52, AT-4, LRAC, Eryx, Milan and the 12.7 mm guns, are used during the firing and movement lessons.

The firing sessions are made all the more realistic by the use of sound effects, fireworks and explosions representing the enemy's firing. Cohesion, rapidity in the execution of orders and precision shooting will naturally influence the evaluation of the unit. The counting system relies simply on the number of targets shot down within a given time. CEITO evaluation is naturally an operational test which counts in the career of a captain.

Fires, smoke and flames for the 2nd company in action at the CEITO. All the infantry weapons in the company are used, defensively and offensively
(Yves Debay)

Next page:
NBC attack at the CEITO
(Yves Debay)

1st company insignia

During a course at Hammelburg, searching a house is carried out with the help of the Dog Platoon.
(Yves Debay)

During the specialisation which was brought in at the beginning of the sixties, the training of the 1st company is given over to anti-tank and night fighting, but over the years the unit has specialised in sector work. Most modern operations take place in urban areas like the recent operations in Bangui and Brazzaville. Apart from the CEC (Centre d'Entraînement Commando - Commando training centre) which are spread out all over France and which have all the necessary facilities, the company can also use the combat village at Frasseli, in Corsica. Once a year, the unit gets training enabling it to invest buildings and reduce enemy resistance in an urban environment. Moreover, every year the 1st company of the 2e REP goes to Hammelburg, the famous Bundeswehr's combat village. At the end of this annual course, the young legionaries receive a Certificat technique Elémentaire.

Discovering the fortified positions of Beyhum square in Beirut, set up by the Palestinians during Operation Epaulard was a real shock for the French

units. This experience was of benefit to company instructors and officers who now use traditional investigative methods and up-to-date methods in urban contexts. Armament is adapted to missions in this environment and the 1st company is equipped with 12 Remington shotguns. Plastic ammunition with 9-ball buckshotand Brenneke (ammunition) used together with a gas cartridge, which is particularly effective.

Each combat section has a FAMAS equipped with a laser indicator. Apart from the psychological impact when the red spot is easily seen on the target, this system is very effective for indicating targets, particularly on the side of buildings. The company works a lot at night and discretely, and 12 FAMAS have been equipped with silencers.

The officers would like to have disposable flame-throwers like some shock units in the Russian army. In town fighting, this could turn out to be a formidable weapon.

Modular ladders and the aluminium 'Puga' kit ladder are being tested a together with grapnel launchers. The Legion paratroopers of the 1st company are obviously specialised in the use of rope and can also abseil.

Apart from its three combat platoons and its support platoon, the 1st company has a dog platoon. The dogs are used on guard for the Raffalli barracks in Calvi, but their use in town combat is nowadays very common, especially in tracking.

In the modern history of the regiment, the 'Greens' were engaged during Operation *Isk-outir* (Djibouti), in Sarajevo, Bangui and in 1997 in Brazzaville where two legionaries were seriously wounded. In Spring 2000, after a course on maintaining law and order at la Courtine, the company was sent to Kosovo where its know-how turned out to be very useful in Mitrovica.

Top:
After jumping over the airport at Figari, in the south of Corsica, legionaries from the 1st company rejoin their fighting positions. This is the type of exercise which prepares them for the big adventures overseas.
(Yves Debay)

Above:
Brazzaville, June 1997, at the 'Case de Gaulle' to which they have evacuated the foreign nationals, the Legion para-troopers, the 'Greens'get to know a new type of mission. Note the VBL armoured car used by the captain for this mission under fire.
(Yves Debay)

Left:
Mitrovica, Kosovo. The 'greens' protecting the Serbs going to church in the Albanian sector of the town.
(Yves Debay)

At a hundred or so kilometres to the east of Frankfurt, the combat village of Hammelburg is situated in the training grounds of the Germany Infantry School.

All the Bundeswehr Jäger or Panzergrenadier regiments, as well as many NATO units, have the opportunity to do some training in town fighting. The advantage of this particular village over other concrete combat villages which are to be found on training grounds everywhere in Europe is that Hammelburg is a real village. It was emptied of its inhabitants in the thirties for use by the Wehrmacht. The courses are particularly realistic.

The German soldiers have set up some of the houses in the Lebanese style, with interior defences, staircase protection, booby-trapped window sills, etc…

Since 1997 the 1st company, which is twinned with a unit of the German Special Forces, has the opportunity to use the facilities at Hammelburg. Depending on the availability of the company, the course lasts one or two weeks.

Work is done at first in groups, then by sections, then finally by the whole company and all its support sections.

In defence, a section alone can hold a house, but it takes three to invest a small building and a whole battalion to take a whole block. These facts have been confirmed by recent urban combat at Grozni in Chechenia.

At Hammelburg the Legion paratroopers also learn how to fortify a house by setting up firing positions set back from the openings, which makes it even harder for the attackers.

Left:
In urban combat, it is preferable to invest a building if at all possible from above. Other techniques used include abseiling from a helicopter to merely using a ladder… as can be seen in this demonstration made at Hammelburg.
(Yves Debay)

Above:
In closed spaces, shots can come from anywhere, especially from the floors above which have to be watched all the time.
(Yves Debay)

Top right:
Typical example of a defensive position. Well protected, the MINIMI server is invisible from the outside and can scan a whole street practically at point blank range.
(Yves Debay)

Right:
A combat group invests a building. Note the shot-gun which is very useful in this type of situation, and the Miles training simulator. Trials using this type of equipment have shown that in localised fighting, the opponents could suffer 70% losses.
(Yves Debay)

Next page:
At Mitrovica, the old Legion rejoins the modern one with its legionaries armed with big shields resembling the Roman scutum, but made of Plexiglas, keeping law and order oblige.
(Yves Debay)

THE DOG PLATOON

Below:
Above all do not let the 'Dogs of War' loose.
(Yves Debay)

From time immemorial, the dog has accompanied man into battle, and the 2e REP is no exception. At the beginning of the eighties, a dog platoon was attached to the CCS for guard duties around the camp at Raffalli. Things developed very quickly and from October 1994, the dogs were attached to a combat company, the 5th platoon of the first company.

Under the leadership of a dynamic warrant officer, the 2e REP's dog platoon has not only done its bit guarding, but also shown that the 'war dogs' can be a real part of the combat unit set up by the regiment.

Next page:
The 'Dogs of War' training.

Next page centre
This REP dog has just ferreted out a terrorist from his hide-out and will no longer let go. *(Yves Debay)*

Next page bottom
An concrete example of mission: guarding 3rd company Zodiac rubber boats with his master during the Pégase exercise. *(Yves Debay)*

132

Set up with dogs from the *132e Groupe Cynophile des Armées* (army Dog Groups), based at Suippe, the dog platoon is attached to the 1st combat company and is made up of 14 men, each responsible for a dog. These four-legged auxiliaries are Alsatians, and German shepperds and Dutch sheep-dogs. There are three types of missions:

1. Guarding, which is the normal job of the dog platoon. The dogs guard equipment, buildings, vehicles and sometimes help the personnel do the rounds. This type of job is particularly welcome in Africa where dogs are particularly dissuasive for the locals who are always ready to pilfer equipment and supplies.

A dog can also accompany an officer who is carrying important documents. If given the order, the dog will not let anyone get near the briefcase containing the documents.

2. Town fighting. The 1st company increasingly uses a dog team when investigating and searching a building. The dog is not trained to attack an entrenched adversary who would simply shoot it; it helps rather to locate the enemy especially when he is deeply dug in in lairs, underground passages, sewers and cellars which are as many deadly traps.

3. Keeping law and order. Held by long leads and wearing a special muzzle, the dogs can be released against dangerous individuals or at leaders of a demonstration. The charge by a 2e REP 'War Dog' can knock out a fully-equipped soldier.

In the 2e REP, the Dog platoon is a very special unit, enthusiastic and full of bites.

Below
Part of the Dog platoon posing with animals which also have the qualities of the legionary: loyalty and bite.
(Yves Debay)

Left:
Concentration and effort can be seen on the faces of these legionaries from the 2nd company, carrying out a mountaineering exercise. Climbing a cliff with weapons and a 20-kilo backpack is far from easy.
(Yves Debay)

Next page:
On order to train its Legionaries, the 2nd REP has the magnificent site at Golo, not far from Calvi. *(Yves Debay)*

Inset next page:
Climbing session in the rocks at Golo.
(Yves Debay)

Botom: **On a rocky peak overlooking la Balagne, Legion paratroopers of the 2nd company get their equipment ready for an abseiling session.**
(Yves Debay)

2nd compagny insigna

At the end of the eighties and before the Army became professional, the 2nd company of the 2e REP, was the only professional company specialised in mountain warfare in the French Army. Nowadays, the missions are the same, and the *'Reds'* continue developing their capability of operating in bad weather and on mountainous terrain.

By 'bad weather' is meant operating in winter in snow and by *'mountainous terrain'* crossing and climbing mountains, but also difficult built-up areas.

To carry out these two missions, the company has developed two types of know-how. Firstly *'remaining stationary'*, holding out in the mountain. To do this the legionaries learn to live in an igloo, learn to build snow shelters, move vertically with the help of rope and move horizontally by using cross-country skis.

Secondly, the use of weapons and fighting in the mountains. In this dangerous environment, characterised by deeply enclosed areas, where a platoon can pin down a whole company, the 2nd company learns how to hold a point and stay there. Individual weapons are of course used but for more long distance shooting, the old AA-52 is still very effective. Heavy sniping is being developed using the Barett, MacMillan and PGM rifles, cumbersome of course, but oh how effective in the *'War of the Crests'*.

For training, the 2nd company has the use of the Vergio chalet in Corsica and the marvellous Golo mountain climbing areas in Corsica as well as a chalet at Montgenèvre, near Briançon, lent to them by the Alpine Brigade with whom there are frequent exchanges. Officer training lasts 22 weeks, eleven in winter and eleven in summer, at the Chamonix moun-

(Following text p. 138)

DIFFICULT PASSAGES

In the case of an engagement taking place over difficult or mountainous terrain, it is the 2nd Company which spearheads the regiment, reconnoitres the difficult passages and marks out the path for the rest of the REP. The 2nd company can also attempt to infiltrate behind the enemy lines by unidentified and inaccessible paths. In order to carry out these different missions, the 2nd company must practice mountaineering as and when the opportunities, mission included, present themselves.

FIGHTING IN WINTER

THE CICEM
Moving around, living and fighting 2 000 metres up or in very low temperatures are some of the specialities of the 2nd Company. This know-how has been learnt and kept up during winter training courses at Vergio in Corsica or Montgenèvre near Briançon. The Legion paratroopers also take the mountain combat certificate which rewards three very intensive weeks' activity at the CICEM (*Centre d'Instruction au Combat en Montagne/mountain fighting instruction and training centre*) at Barcelonette.

Previous page top:
**Winter training course
at Vergio.**

Previous page, bottom:
**Moving about quickly on skis,
during a winter training course
at Montgenèvre.
Speed in execution of shooting
and movement is a guarantee
of success in all climates.**
(Yves Debay)

**In the mountain as in the jungle,
transporting a casualty
can immobilise a platoon.**
(Yves Debay)

**Fighting in extreme conditions
is the 'privilege'
of the 2ᵉ Compagnie.**
(Yves Debay)

Right:
**A moving around and shooting
on skis exercise at Vergio
in Corsica.**
(Yves Debay)

tain training school. One of the last unit commanders was a mountain guide. Some officers are of Swiss or Austrian origin and obviously share their natural know-how with their fellow legionaries.

Soldier training comprises two sessions, first the BAM (Brevet Alpin Militaire - Military Mountain Certificate) in summer taken during a three-week training course in Corsica; and second the BSM (Brevet de skieur militaire - Military Skiing Certificate) obtained at the end of a winter training course.

Legionaries from Ivory Coast or Cambodia obtained their certificates without much trouble from the physical point of view and by dint of willpower. When taking the BSM, the first week is given over to learning to ski and the Legion Paratroopers without previous experience in this matter learn very quickly to move along with the 'peau de phoque' *(Seal skins: ski shealth to make the skis slide more quietly)*, carrying packs and weapons. The second week is given over to learning mountain fighting and the third is an end-of-course recapitulation exercise with a tactical theme and naturally the application of mountain combat techniques. Needless to say that all these training periods are all very trying both physically and morally, the effect of the cold combining with the intense physical effort.

To get his BAM, the legionary has to climb up and down 1000 metres in less than 3.30 hours over 15 kilometres. Only 15 minutes are allowed for the descent and the average for the company is 2.20 hours which just shows how very fit the legionaries really are. Parachute jumps into over snow also carried out.

The corporals and lance-corporals can also obtain the Diplôme Supérieur de Chef de Cordée (Higher certificate for mountain group leaders) for winter/summer. The mountain is a hard school and the 2nd company was able to put its specialised training to good effect during Operation Salamandre in Bosnia, where a number of ski patrols were carried out on Mount Igman to check up on the implementation of the Daytona Agreements.

The 2nd company also distinguished itself during the hostage taking at Loyada in Djibouti and during Operation Requin (Shark) in Gabon.

Right and next page:
After being transported by Zodiacs of the 3rd company, the 'Reds' climbed a cliff at night and are now well-positioned. They are approaching the citadel of Bonifacio to seize it during the *Pégase 98* exercise. The REP is versatile and can just as well take a classic defensive position during an NBC attack as special operations.
(Yves Debay)

THE THIRD 'AMPHIBIOUS' COMPANY

3rd company insignia

Poseidon's trident is the symbol of the 3rd company specialised in everything to do with water and especially the reconnaissance and the capture of beaches. The amphibious company includes 5 officers, 23 NCOs and 123 legionaries.

Before being specialists with rubber boats and flippers, the men of the 3rd company are first of all elite infantry.

The company, like all the others, is made up of three combat platoons and one support platoon, but for its amphibious activities, these elements can be changed into underwater reconnaissance platoon, or into sea transort platoon and landingplatoon.

The unit is naturally the regiment's spearhead if the regimentis called upon to do this type of amphibious mission.

Amphibious training is done in phases and there are two specialisations: reconnaissance diver for beach reconnaissance, and boarding master. By day or night, the legionaries operate the company's Zodiac rubber boats.

There are 15 training and 15 10- man 40hp transport Zodiac boats. For the end-of-training course recapitulation exercise, a round tour of the island of Corsica is made in rubber boats punctuated by approaches and coast raids. Navigation by compass and GPS are also part of the training.

Once trained, the men from the 3rd company carry out numerous water exercises and once or twice a year, take part in joint exercises with the Navy. Parachute jumps into the sea, drops from 'Super Frelon' helicopters, dropping divers from submarines or Zodiac raids from Navy surface vessels are part of the programme.

At Calvi, the 3rd company runs and maintains the amphibious centre.

The staff is also called upon to follow diving courses at the Army diving school at Angers. The elementary level lasts 13 weeks, the 1st level 6 weeks and the 2nd a year.

Some members also qualify for the IO (Intervention Offensive - Attack and Intervention) and the company can muster a team at short notice. Even if the regiment does not have any, the men know how to use the Oxygair diving equipment.

Apart form its amphibious missions, the 3rd company takes part in operations abroad and has distinguished itself in Chad, Djibouti during Operation Godoria, in Somalia during Operation 'Restore Hope', in ex-Yugoslavia and recently in Bangui during Operation *Aladdin 2*. Its last operational deployment was at Mitrovica in Kosovo.

ZODIAC RAIDS

These are used intensively by both the Marine Commandos and the 3rd company of the 2e REP. Zodiac raiding is a discreet infiltration technique in order to harass unprotected coasts. This type of rapid surprise operation can help set up a amphibious bridgehead by protecting the flanks of the landing beaches.

This type of raid is carried out normally at night, launched from a submarine or from a fast and discreet ship. Launched 50 kilometres from the coast, the Zodiacs refuel at sea and reach their rallying point as quickly as possible, usually a quiet creek where the men land to carry out their mission.

Top right:
Once landed by Zodiac, parachute, or helicopter as is the case here, during *Pégase 98*, the legionaries from the 3e company are used as pure infantrymen.
(Yves Debay)

Right and next page:
Zodiacs launched from the surveillance ship *Mérou* have just landed a platoon of the 3rd company on a beach in Corsica. The 'Blacks' check their equipment before moving off to filter inland.
(Yves Debay)

RECONNAISSANCE DIVERS

Diver insignia

Below:
The company also jumps into the sea.
(Sergent-chef Phillips - 2ᵉ REP)

Situated at a few yards from the coast, the Centre Amphibie (Amphibious Centre) of the 2ᵉ REP, attached to the 3rd company, is in charge of training amphibious specialists from the REP as well as looking after and storing all the equipment necessary for this specialisation. The PAT team is also stationed here. Their mission is to infiltrate quietly with flippers or kayaks to check if a beach is mined or protected by the enemy. If this is the case, the swimmers will eliminate all opposition in order to make a Zodiac raid or a landing all the easier. In spite of what many authors have written, and even if some officers have followed IO specialisation courses, the REP does not have any combat divers. Combat divers are the domain only of the Navy, and particularly the Hubert Commando.

However, now that the regiment has been mechanised, a SAF *(Section d'Aide au Franchissement/a platoon for help in crossing obstacles)* has been set up in order to help VABs when they encounter an obstacle which somehow has to be crossed

There are three levels to the training given by the Centre Amphibie.

Level 1 (Bronze): 15 days where the legionaries learn to steer a 6-man 9 hp Zodiac, to swim 4 kms with flippers in less than two hours, do a bit of hand-to-hand fighting and learn the basic tactical procedures for amphibious operations.

Level 2 (Silver): This is carried out at platoon level. The legionaries learn how to steer a 10-man 40 hp Zodiac. Training includes 8 kms swimming with flippers in less than four hours, serious hand-to-hand fighting training which could come in useful during a raid, as well as a lot of tactical exercises enabling the team to carry out the amphibious operations procedures correctly.

Level 3 (Gold): This course is a condensed version of the first two and the legionary who succeeds in passing it will be able to do all the amphibious centre missions. This course is primarily for learning to use and navigate with a kayak. Those who pass the course can also be posted to the Centre Amphibie.

Various methods used by the reconnaissance divers of the 2e REP to infiltrate or exfiltrate, notably dropping into the sea from a Navy helicopter.
(Yves Debay)

Reconnaissance divers can also infiltrate by kayak. A Nautiraid kayak is used; it has two big waterproof bags with a capacity of 60kg. A kayak ready for war with two legionaries aboard weighs 300 kilos. *(Yves Debay)*

4th company insigna.

Previous page:
**3 levels' insignia
from the 'Centre Amphibie'.**

Below:
**Practically invisible
on the edges of the undergrowth,
this tree-man counter-sniper team
can strike out at a distance of one
kilometre. The photo was taken in
Bosnia in the summer of 1999,
a theatre of operations where
the 4e's know-how turned out
to be very useful.**
(Yves Debay)

At Kolwezi, snipers had shown how effective they could be and ever since then the 2e REP has favoured this type of action which is less costly than a classic infantry assault and which can be psychologically very effective, especially in Africa. The Balkan conflicts, particularly the interposition operations in Sarajevo also demonstrated the value of counter-snipers.

Fighting behind enemy lines and using snipers and explosive experts are the domain of the 4th company. As weapon experts, the 'Greys', when they are not abroad on a mission, are present on all the shooting ranges, either as snipers or destruction experts. Their knowledge of weapons is such that the DIA (Direction de l'inspection des armements/Weapons inspectorate) entrusts them with new equipment for testing before distributing it to the rest of the Army. Minimi, British L-96, Barret MacMillan and Hecate 2 were thus ground tested with the 4th company. Nowadays, the 4th company is very interested in the SM (Super Magnum), a British weapon built by Accuracy International, whose 8.6 mm calibre or 338 magnum is a good compromise between the Cal 12.7 heavy weapons and the regulation FR-F2s.

Telemetry also has place of honour and several types of laser telemetry are also tested. At the moment it is the digital dataTM-18, with a X6 magnification and a range of 10kms which has been selected for the sniping team leaders. Shooting in all its forms is naturally practised by day and night.

In combat, of the Central European sort, the 4th company has been trained to leave small groups of snipers behind the enemy positions to cause panic and havoc before rejoining their own lines by their own means.

French infantry is in the middle of a profound change and the 4th company like all the others in the REP, is a tactical testing ground.

The use of a new type of platoon with three 'voltige' groups, one group with ATK on Eryx, with a support group with *Hecate 2*s was tried out particularly with the 4th before being adopted by the whole of the infantry. Rigour, accuracy of execution and perfect knowledge of all equipment used are the qualities needed by these destruction experts who handle plastic, tolite and TNT just as well at the CNEC at Mont-Louis as at Arta Beach in Djibouti. These Legion paratroopers are also capable of delaying an enemy by littering his advance with a lot of mines and booby traps. There is a very beautiful training room in the company where the different types of mines and all sorts of traps brought back from all around the world can be studied by the legionaries. All these activities did not prevent the 'Greys' of the 4th company from distinguishing themselves at Kolwezi, in Rwanda, at Sarajevo, Bangui and recently in Kosovo.

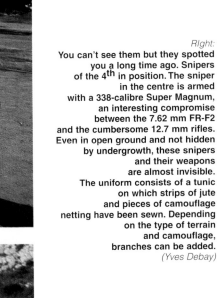

SNIPING

The sniper is a soldier who has always existed, from the Balearic slingshots in the Roman legions to the cross-bowmen of the Middle Ages. It was during the American War of Independence that the modern concept of the sniper waiting in ambush originated, with the Rebels armed with precision rifles shooting at the Red Coats, especially at their officers.

Since then the techniques have evolved a lot and the REP has always been up-to-date in this domain, especially by regrouping its snipers in sections. 25 years' experience of precision shooting and sniping have given the 4th company a unique brand of experience.

During the Cold War and in a defensive fighting context against a mechanised force along an axis, the 4th company was trained to let the enemy go past so that they could leave groups of snipers behind the enemy's lines. These would work in small groups staggered with one team firing and the other acting as fall-back; they could easily hold off a mechanised column for several hours before rejoining their own lines.

In the French Army, the sharpshooter works according to the rules within a platoon whereas the sniper is engaged further away and alone. The 1st platoon of the 4th has 13 FR-F2 snipers whereas there are normally 3 per platoon. Instruction is given within the company and the sniper is the one who is calm and patient; he is a good shot, of course, and has a very good sense of direction, signals and camouflage; he is also capable of operating by himself or in little groups inside the enemy lines.

Training a sniper takes four weeks. The first with a 12.7 calibre rifle, the second and the third on the FR-F2 and Super Magnum and the fourth is a recapitulation including three day's practical work.

Apart from the specialised sections, the legionaries from other companies can also do a proficiency course with the 4th; this means that the regiment always has a reserve of trained sharpshooters. During operation Almandin, the REP's airborne group could have called on 44 snipers without notice, had headquarters wanted.

AGAINST HEAVY SNIPING

1. in Viet-Nam, the US Marines dealt with the Viet-Cong snipers with 106 mm recoilless canon and the Serbs do not hesitate to silence a sniper with a tank or 20 mm triple tubes.

The military always like to say that the best way to counter a tank is with another tank. This is equally true of snipers especially during interposition missions where it is preferable to avoid collateral damage [1]. The first French troops engaged at Sarajevo often found themselves fighting against snipers who were solidly entrenched in hideouts and firing by means of a system of mirrors. Moreover, many of these hideouts were right in the middle of civilian buildings.

Against this type of crafty fighting, the FR-F2s, which are very effective over rural terrain, lack the power to neutralise a well-sheltered enemy sniper. The appearance of a new generation of large calibre precision rifles changed the course of events and the hunter frequently found himself becoming the hunted. One or two 12.7 bullets can easily go through a wall and silence a sniper.

French soldiers in Sarajevo were the first to use this type of weapon, especially the 4th company of the 2e REP, which was a pioneer in the use of heavy precision rifles. The 'Greys' tested and used different models among which the Barret, the Mac Millan and the PGM Hecate, which has now been adopted by the French Army.

TESTING

Being ordered to let off thousands of cartridges is a pleasure they can afford in the 4th company, as it is often chosen to test new equipment in the field, like here, with the new Minimi in 1991.

149

DESTRUCTION

Delaying the enemy by destruction, harassing him by laying mines or traps in the most unexpected places or by getting behind the enemy lines to sabotage communications, buildings or ammunition dumps are all part of the 4e Companie's know-how.

These legionaries can also open the way for the regiment by using explosives.

By combining the murderous fire of snipers and traps and destruction, the 4e Compagnie can considerably delay all enemy progress.

Top right: **On the regimental shooting range to the south of Calvi, young legionaries are taking part in calculation and how to place an explosive charge exercises, thus learning the job of an explosives expert in the 4th.**

Left: **The result of a good calculation is always spectacular.**

Right: **The skills of the explosives experts in the 4th. are often tested during firing exercises. At Larzac, this staff-sergeant from the 4th. is about to set off an unexploded AT-4 warhead.**

Below: **These Legion paratroopers from the 4th are preparing a Bangalore torpedo to open a breach in a network of barbed wire. Even in the year 2000, war can still be classical in some of its aspects.**
(Photos: Yves Debay)

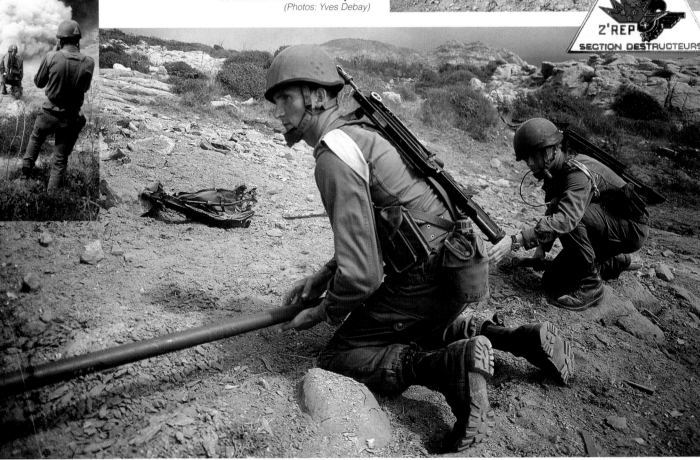

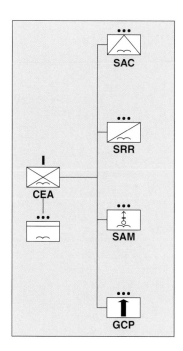

Below:
The CEA gathers together most of the regiment's heavy equipment like this tank breaker's Milan at the beginning of a night exercise at Calvi.
(Yves Debay)

Inset:
CEA insigna

The CEA is the 'muscle' of the regiment and the Corps Commander uses it to 'wage war', because it is its firepower, either used massively or in small doses to help a company, which will make all the difference.

The assault on Vrbanja, but also a few well-placed 120 mm mortar shots made the belligerents in Bosnia realise that the tide had turned. In this same context the CEA of the 2e REP is a very effective, formidable force, and its use with all its heavy means in any high-or low-density conflict would be significant.

The 2e REP's CEA is organised in the same way as all the other units of the same type belonging to the French Infantry; in the REP, it has 8 officers, 40 NCOs and 105 legionaries.

There are an anti-tank platoon, a six-piece heavy mortarplatoonn, a reconnaissance platoon, a command platoon and the GCP (Groupe de Commandos Parachutistes).

The restructuring of the Army has cost the CEA an anti-tank platoon and the anti-aircraft platoon with its 20 mm canon.

Because of its diversity and its different types of missions, the CEA is a difficult company to command, but the captain commanding the unit can count on his officers who not only have a lot of experience but also the calm of older soldiers.

For more than thirty years, the men in the CEA have been engaged everywhere where combat has reared its head, either with all the means at their disposal, or sometimes as simple paratroopers, since the CEA is often used as an ordinary combat company.

The CEA's mission is to give the regiment with support from its 120 mm mortars; the CEA is also the regiment's eyes thanks to its reconnaissance platoon and its GCP working behind enemy lines.

The servers of these heavy weapons have been trained within the regiment at CTE level, training in the camps in Champagne or at Canjuers.

The company was one of the first in France to receive the new 81 mm mortars, which complement the 120s, but which are easier to use, especially in the African theatre of operations which the regiment knows well.

The GCP platoon (*Groupement des Commandos Parachutistes*) is one of the finest jewels of the regiment and is responsible to the CEA.

Within the REP, the CEA is without doubt the company which has the widest variety of types of missions but it has a very likeable 'calm strength' about it.

The CEA has been engaged in all theatres of operations often as an ordinary marching company without its heavy equipment as was the case in Brazzaville and in Bosnia.

Top:
The famous GCP, one of the 2e REP's prides,
are attached to the CEA. Here the GCPs
get their equipment ready before a free fall jump.

Center:
Other climes, other means of diplomacy.
The men of the SAM have abandoned their mortars
to set up a checkpoint in Bosnia and search
a Bosnian Serb army lorry.

Below:
The Legion paratroopers sometimes have
to be very diplomatic. Here it is obviously necessary to talk!
With a rather frozen smile, this CEA NCO tries to explain
to this quite clearly drugged Cobra militiaman that it would be
good idea to take the Chinese grenade out of his mouth.
The scene took place during Operation *Pelican* in Brazzaville.
(Photos Yves Debay)

REGIMENTAL RECONNAISSANCE PLATOON (SRR)

On the front line the SRR is one of the first means of intelligence gathering which the regiment has and often the whole regimental headquarters depends upon it.

Commanded nowadays by a warrant-officer, the SRR is made up of 5 NCOs and 25 legionaries. Its mission is not to give battle but to gather information about enemy troops and their movements and to look for the fault in the enemy's defensive lay-out so as to be able to exploit it.

In the case of engagement with the enemy the SRR, which is entirely motorised with 10 P-4s, must immediately disengage by taking advantage of its firepower. This is impressive because it includes MILANs, ERYXs and AT-4 for anti-tank work, together with 12.7 mm and 7.62 mm machine guns for dealing with unprotected objectives. Each Legion paratrooper in the SRR is of course a specialist in identifying armoured vehicles and is well-versed in the art of camouflage. All the vehicles are equipped with frequency-avoiding PR-4G radio sets

and each man is equipped with night sights. The platoon is divided into one command patrol with two P-4s, one of which is armed with a 12.7 mm machine gun, one support patrol with two MILAN-equipped P-4s and three scout patrols. These are each equipped with two p-4s, one with a 12.7 mm machine gun and an ERYX, the other armed with a 7.62 mm machine gun and an AT-4. The CEA's firepower is therefore considerable because for ten vehicles there are four 12.7 mm and four 7.62 mm machines guns, two Milan firing positions, two for ERYX, four AT-4s and 31 FAMASs.

Left:
A reconnaissance patrol has been caught at full speed during a non tactical sortie -the vehicles are totally uncovered.
(Yves Debay)

Below: **Perfectly camouflaged at the edge of the undergrowth, the two P-4s from the SRR show two types of machine guns used: the AA-52 and the Browning M-2.** *(Yves Debay)*

THE ANTI-TANK PLATOON

With the reorganising of the French Army, the CEA lost one of its anti-tank sections. Nevertheless, the SAC *(Section Anti-char/Anti-tank Platoon)* still has heavy firepower with its six MILAN firing positions, which if placed judiciously can destroy a squadron of battle tanks.

The platoon is composed of a command group with two 4x4 P-4 vehicles and three anti-tank combat groups.

The anti-tank combat group consists of two P-4s with two firing positions and 12 missiles in reserve. These are MILAN F-2Ts of the new generation, with a tandem hollow charge capable of pulverising any modern battle tank. These missiles are equipped with an anti-jamming device. If the regiment is motorised, the SAC can obviously fire its missiles from the VABs or use the new Sovamag in the case of a parachute operation.

The platoon also has a firing simulator to train future tank busters as well as those from other companies. There are two firing positions per combat company.

Above:
**A MILAN simulator session.
The servers are trained within
the regiment.**
(Yves Debay)

Right:
**During the Pegasus 98 exercise,
this anti-tank group,
very well camouflaged in the Corsican
undergrowth is ready to block
this road to any armoured vehicle.
The MILAN has a range of 2 000m**
(Yves Debay)

MILAN

Missile weight: 6,65 kg.
Launcher weight: 16,4 kg. **Range:**
2 000 m.
Maximum flight time: 12,5 secondes.
Speed: 200 m/s.

**The lastest Milan warhead can
destroy any present day combat
tank.**

Previous page, top:
**A Milan-equipped P-4 from the SAC
during range-finding exercise.**
(Yves Debay)

Previous page, bottom:
**Once a year at Canjuers Camp,
the SAC is tested operationally
by the infantry inspection.
Part of the shooting is carried out
under NBC conditions.**
(Yves Debay)

MORTAR SUPPORT PLATOON

Ever since the legendary exploits of the Foreign Legion's heavy mortar sections during Indochina, the legionaries serving the mortars have always had the confidence of the regiment. Everybody knows that in the case of a company being in a tight spot, they will be there and that they can be counted upon to surround a threatened company with protective fire… and 120 mm shells fired in rapid succession hurt a lot. The platoon is now called SAM *(Section d'Appui Mortier/Mortar support Platoon)* instead of the older SMI *(Section de Mortier Lourd/heavy mortar Platoon)* includes teams which serve six 120 mm Thomson-Brandt tubes, one firing preparation team and two liaison and observation teams who can direct the fire from a forward position.

The 120 mms can be parachuted on a pallet with their mule; or transported by helicopter in a sling by ALAT Pumas or Navy Super Frelons; or towed behind a VAB when the regiment is motorised. It was thus that the SAM was used in Bosnia in 1995.

The CEA was also one of the first companies in the Army to receive the new LLR *(Long Léger Renforcé/long light and reinforced)* 81 mm mortars. They are parachuted in a GC-23 bundle with six shots immediately available and are easier to use than the 120 mm. During an airborne mission, 70 shots are available per gun and delivered in a drop parcel. Whether with the 120 or with the LLR, the SAM legionaries are particularly effective. They are nevertheless very familiar with infantry work since during operation Pelican in Brazzaville and during their most recent deployment in Bosnia, they worked as pure infantrymen.

Left:
Young legionaries from the CEA trying new 81 mm rocket launching mortars at the Larzac training camp firing range.
(Yves Debay)

Bottom left.
Night firing session at la Courtine camp
(Sergent-chef Phillips - 2ᵉ REP)

Bottom right:
With a view to its deployment in Bosnia, the SAM did a shooting camp at la Courtine.
(Sergent-chef Phillips - 2ᵉ REP)

THE PARACHUTE COMMANDO GROUPE (GCP)

Linked to the CEA for administrative and management reasons, the GCPs take their orders directly from the BOI *(Bureau Opération Instruction/Operations and instruction office)*, the regimental headquarters. Where air training is concerned, it is brigade headquarters which manages the jump sessions. For operational reasons, the REPs GCPs can also be regrouped with their colleagues in other parachute regiments in the brigade for a particular mission, as was the case with the capture of Al-Salman fort in Iraq during Operation *Daguet*.

These elite soldiers are mostly officers recruited among the NCOs and the corporals of the regiment; they have thus at least four years' service behind them. After very trying physical tests, they are trained very intensively in all domains related to fighting of a high level. Tactical training is carried out in the regiment, but there are a lot of selection tests and proficiency tests in different instruction centres. A GCP must be certified by the CNEC at Mont-Louis as a second level commando monitor. The training of a professional parachutist is given at the ETAP (Ecole des Troupes aéroportées - Airborne troops training school) at Pau. They can also intervene in hostage rescue operations and because of this, they sometimes take part in training sessions with the GIGN.

Their main mission within the regiment is the help they give to the regiment when it is to be engaged or about to be landed, which can be translated by a 'seize and hold' operation within an airborne context, a reconnaiss`ance mission behind enemy lines or the classic pathfinder mission, marking out a landing zone. Other missions include looking for people like war criminals, intelligence gathering or getting foreign nationals out.

The GCP can also intervene in special actions like in Yugoslavia in 1995 or side by side with American Special Forces when the GCPs of the REP neutralised an islamist commando training centre.

To carry out these varied functions, the GCP has 27-30 men divided into six cells. Two ten-man operational teams are ready to go on a mission at a moment's notice, 24h/24h. The different cells are: command, health, signals, operational technique, shooting-mines-explosives and photographic intelligence.

The technical operational cell apart from its planning work, is also a testing ground for new methods in the tactical domain and in the use of the GCPs.

Equipment and weapons are specific like the Questar lenses for long-distance day sighting. Weapons are chosen according to the mission. Apart from the laser-sighted FAMAS, the GCPs use shot guns and Heckler and Koch MP-5machine pistols with silencers. Planes, helicopters, ast vehicles, submarines… and, often overlooked, simple walking are the principal means of infiltration and exfiltration.

Below:
In order to infiltrate, all means are useful including submarines. Here Galatée has rendez-voused with a GCP team at sea. In a few moments the Zodiac s will be loaded and the sub will dive and then drop the night commando again on a quiet bit of coast. These photographs are old and theoretically, infiltration by submarine is the province of the Navy commandos. Nevertheless, if the case arises, the GCP can carry out this type of mission.
(Yves Debay)

157

Above:
GCPs embarking for a commando jumping exercise session. The 'all on the back' parachute seems to be light but the harness seems to be a lot less. *(Yves Debay)*

Left:
One of the most classic missions for the GCPs is reconnoitring and marking landing zones, here during the *Winged Crusader 96* exercise where the GCPs are in contact with the planes in the second wave. *(Yves Debay)*

Bottom left an next page:
Thanks to their chutes the GCPs can approach silently, right onto the zone to be dealt with, and land on a handkerchief. As opposed to the automatic parachute opening of the big airborne operations, regrouping is not a problem. The GCPs have G-9 wings which have replaced the CQ-360. *(Yves Debay)*

Bottom:
To fulfil its missions and fight in cramped surroundings, the GCPs are specially equipped with weapons like this H 1 K MP-5 with a silencer and laser sights, or a Mossberg or Remington pump-action shotgun. Each soldier also has a Beretta automatic pistol. *(Yves Debay)*

Bottom right:
The GCPs take part of course in all the regiment's missions. Here during *Almandin 2* a team is checking that some dugouts have not been used to supply the rebels. *(Yves Debay)*

HALO/HAHO Jumper's insignia

DIRECT SIGNALS

Thanks to a portable computer and a digital camera, the GCPs can send pictures of the objective or of the jump zone directly. In this era of satellites, human intelligence gathering is still very important. One of the special points of the REP's GCPs is their use of a digital camera capable of sending back photos taken during a reconnaissance mission directly to the regimental command post. For example, the operator takes a series of photos of buildings of a little African airport in which hostile units are entrenched; the shots are transmitted thanks to a portable computer, encrypted to the regimental command post. Thanks to this method, the assault sections who are going to attack afterwards will know the lie of the land exactly. This method is used also to locate hostage takers.

The parachute drop is the principal means of infiltration of the GCPs. There are three types of jumps: the classic jump with automatic release from a low-flying plane, the HALO (High Altitude, Low Opening) where the parachutist himself opens the chute after a free fall, and the HAHO (High Altitude, High Opening) where the GCPs open the parachutes as soon as they leave the plane and start a long penetration by parachute.

This very up-to-date method is obviously done at night; the GCPs see each other by means of night-glasses and a GPS (Global Positioning System) instrument giving their position to the nearest foot thanks to a satellite. These methods enable teams to be infiltrated very discreetly indeed.

The REP's GCPs train intensively for anti-terrorist and hostage rescuing operations. This type of mission is not for use in Metropolitan France as that is the work of the Gendarmerie and the Police, but for overseas and in an operational context.

The GCPs can use approach and anti-terrorist methods in an urban environment to neutralise an enemy command post or free prisoners or hostages.

At the sharp edge of the regiment's special operations, the men in the GCPs of the 2e REP are nevertheless simple in speech and acts. Among them the Master-Sergeant of Moroccan origin who likes to say:

'We are not cowboys, just soldiers and above all legionaries!'

A hotel bombed out by the FNLC is an excellent training ground for the GCPs who can put into practice their knowledge of anti-terrorist methods [1]. This type of exercise is very tiring as it involves permanent nervous tension. They have their fingers constantly on triggers and they have to be able to react instantly in a co-ordinated manner. An exchange of shots in a cramped space can be very deadly and can lead to mistakes. Terrorists exchange their clothes for those of the hostages and use them as human shields. Note the night vision glasses and the uniforms which are similar to those of the GIGN except that they are camouflaged.
(Yves Debay)

1. The photographs and the vocabulary used on this page must not lead to confusion. The REP's GCPs are not an anti-terrorist unit, because this work is done by the Gendarmerie Nationale. Nevertheless several approach and investigative techniques can be used in the military domain especially during commando operations aiming for instance to neutralise an enemy command post.

5th COMPANY, SHOCK SPECIALISTS!

Above:
This young legionary is servicing an FR-F2. Radios, weapons, optics, computers, NBC systems can be serviced in the 'fifth'.
(Yves Debay)

This unit is one of the most recent in the 2e REP. Created on 1 August 1994, it has taken up the traditins of th 5e CMRLE *(Compagnie Moyenne de Réparation de la Légion Etrangère/the Foreign Legion's medium repairs company)* which distinguished itself in Indochina.

Following the disbanding of the equipment platoon at Corte in 1994, The need for having specialists in Corsica was satisfied by the 5e Compagnie, a maintenance unit within the 2e REP. Nowadays the 5e Compagnie's mission is to ensure second level (NTI 2) technical support for all the units stationed or in transit in Corsica, and first level support (NTI 1) for the 2e REP.

The company also ensures support for the regiment during overseas exercises and operations.

This type of unit only exists overseas or in very special regiments like those using Leclerc tanks. In the infantry, the 2e REP is the only regiment to have the advantage of integrated support teams (faster reaction time, no wasted time, mutual understanding between the mechanics and the companies being supported, specialists permanently available, etc.)

The soldiers in the 5e Compagnie are partly legionaries from the combat companies who have some technical qualificationss and partly soldiers from the equipment unit who already have a lot of experience of operational support. This rather original mixture means that the

5e Compagnie has a rather special spirit within the 2e REP. Dynamism and energy rubbing shoulders with calm and precision, like all great technicians. It has a strength of three officers and 130 legionaries. All are of course qualified and have three to four years' combat company service before joining the 5e Compagnie, which explain the unit's maturity.

The 5e Compagnie is organised into 5 platoons commanded by a captain.
— A command platoon *(SCdt)*.
— A drivers and maintenance co-ordinating platoon *(SCM)*.
— A mobile platoon to support light and armoured vehicles *(SMOB)*.
— A signals, optical, NBC, small arms, survival and rescue material repair platoon *(SRAT)*.
— A supply platoon *(SAP)*.
— A parachute equipment repairs, maintenance and folding platoon *(SREPP)*.

As can be gathered, from he ERYX missile to the radio to the lase-equipped VAB and the parachutes, the 5e Compagnie can repair just about anything. The 5e Compagnie personnel have taken part in all the regiment's missions since 1994 Chad, Bosnia, Gabon, Congo, New Caledonia, Kosovo and Djibouti.

The legionaries serving in the 5e Compagnie are also qualified in infantry combat techniques that they can reinforce the other companies if needs be.

Above: **This mechanic from the 5e Compagnie has been caught in action with his nose in this VBL armoured car's engine. This is taking place at Raljovac, in Bosnia and even if the VBL is not used by the 2e REP, the legionaries of the 5th company, can repair it.**
(Yves Debay)

Left: **Having his hands all covered in engine oil doesn't prevent the 5e Compagnie's legionaries from being fighters. In the case of problems, the unit can be considered as a regimental reserve which can be parachuted if necessary.**
(Yves Debay)

THE 2e REP'S STOCK OF PARACHUTE

- 1 500 back parachutes (OA) TAP 69626 ÉPI.
- 800 front parachutes (OA) TAP 511.
- 50 miscellaneous 'sails' for equipment drops (OA).
- 80 training 'wings' (OR) PUE 131-32 for the jumpers.
- 30 operational 'wings' (OR) COQ 360 for the parachute commando groups.
- 40 operational 'wings' (OR) G-9 for the parachute commando groups.

Top left and centre left:
A legionary from the 2nd Company on a folding course, working in the drying tower. Even if they have not been used for a jump over the sea, the parachutes must be hung and dried before being folded
(Yves Debay)

Bottom left:
A SREPP officer in action. The folders must work with care and speed and must always bear in mind the fact a comrade's life hangs on their work.
(Yves Debay)

Bottom right:
A womand NCO sewing a 'sail'.
(Yves Debay)

Within the 5e companie, the SREPP *(section de réparation, d'entretien et de pliage des matériels de parachutage/Parachute equipment repairs, maintenance and folding platoon)* is a very special and unique platoon in the 2e REP. It is made up of five MATPARA- trained NCOs and sixteen legionaries, it hosts 15 legionaries from the combat companies who take a 'folding' qualification exam for one month followed by one month's practical application

The SREPP's task is to distribute, control, repair, fold and stock all the speciality's equipment. Every year, an average of 16 000 parachutes of six different types — 1 200 a month — are aired, dried checked, folded reconditioned and stored. The folding course for legionaries last five weeks.

One the know-how has been acquired the trainee folds a parachute and then goes and jumps with it! Once he reaches the ground, he is given the title of 'folder'.

During the following six weeks, he works in the platoon watched by monitors, increasing his production rate with a colleague (two work together on the folding table) and fold 27 parachutes in six hours.

Thanks to this system, the 2e REP has a reserve of men trained in parachute folding and can thus manage its own supply of equipment. In this platoon that the only women wearing the 'béret vert' are to be found.

They are fully-fledged members of the regiment, four repairers under the command of a female adjudant sew the 'sails' and the harnesses back-up when they are damaged in jumps…

163

THE COMMAND AND LOGISTICS COMPANY

CCL insigna.

Without the CCL, the 2ᵉ REP would be a body without a soul. The CCL is the regiment's fan belt and in the Legion paratroopers, the 'Yellows' have a considerable role to play. The company puts at the disposal of the commanding officer everything he needs for his command particularly where signals and logistics are concerned. In the regimental command post, there are three big subdivisions: t*he Bureau Opération Instruction* (BOI), the personnel office and the health service. Its official mission is command function support and logistical supplies. On the ground, during an operation, the tactical EMT (Headquarters) is naturally commanded by a group of men who are trusted implicitly by the Corps commander and who come from CCL. Signals is one of the principal activities of the CCL on the ground; it can run two tactical command posts.

In February 200, in order to satisfy the demands of the new Army 2002-style, the CCS has become the CCL. Apart from losing part of its strength to the new Compagnie de Base et d'Instruction - Basic instruction company, the CBI, the CCL's missions have been refocused on command and logistics.

Being in the CCL does not mean not being in the heart of the action, as was the case of Warrant-Officer Boudissa and the Surgeon-Major who were heavily machine gunned in the VLRA ambulance during the ambush on 6 June 1997 in Brazzaville. The strength of his helmet, which took a direct hit, saved the warrant-officer's life.

The biggest part of the unit is mobile and follows the rest of the regiment on its operations (see organigramme). The CCL's strength is 28 officers, 32 NCOs and 102 legionaries.

As its friendly captain says 'its function is to be present at the right time, the right place with the right quantities of supplies'.

Right: **It is by the name of UCL (Unité de Commandement et de Logistique - Logistics and command unit) that the CCL is known when the regiment is deployed on operation. Here, a shot of the 2ᵉ REP's HQ at the 'trailer factory' at Mitrovica during the regimen's deployment in spring. Note the presence of computers, needed to store all the information from intelligence gathering. The CCL has a computer platoon.** *(Yves Debay)*

In the field, the CCL, apart from its signals mission, supplies the men with food, ammunition and fuel. Its immediate logistical capability is: personnel: 358 men; fuel supplies: 15 M³ trucks; freight supplies 78 tonnes. Thanks to the 2 ambulance VABs, the 'Yellows' can evacuate 10 casualties under fire. Because of it capabilities, the CCL takes part in all aspects of the action.

Because of its signals function, it is on the front line by transmitting information to the tactical command. Through the supplies and support function, it guarantees the regiment freedom of movement.

Right:
Alert at Raljovac! Following the alarm being given, the 'Yellows' have rushed into the shelters and are getting ready to defend headquarters. When needed, the CCL's Legion paratroopers become fighters again. *(Yves Debay)*

Below:
Wearing their 'Ninja Turtle' gear and carrying weapons, these Legion paratroopers fill up an HQ VAB during the latest deployment of the regiment in Bosnia. *(Yves Debay)*

Bottom: **As they are more often at Calvi than the legionaries in the other combat companies, the 'yellows' can get in more jumping practice.** *(Yves Debay)*

THE MILITARY POLICE

The 'Police Militaire' (PM) is based in the citadel at Calvi and is responsible to the CCL; the military police is entrusted with ensuring discipline in the regiment, and is made up of 1 NCO and 9 legionaries using four P-4s.

The inhabitants of Calvi are very familiar with these vehicles marked 'Police Militaire' and the legionaries, who drive them, with their white képis and green and red armband. Every night, the MPs drive round the streets of Calvi making sure everything is all right and rounding up any stray legionaries at closing time. The policemen can also take part in overseas operations by sending a detachment.

There is a story that tells of an enormous black MP corporal in the REP who succeeded in disciplining the journalists besieging the 'PTT building', the UN headquarters, during the worst moments of the Sarajevo siege.

Left:
Every evening the Mps are out. Incidents in Calvi between legionaries and local customers are very rare. *(Yves Debay)*

Next page:
Ensuring communication between the combat companies and the regimental HQ is one of the main missions of the CCL. Here inside an HQ VAB during an operation. Note the insignia of the Salamander Division above the Tricolore armband. *(Yves Debay)*

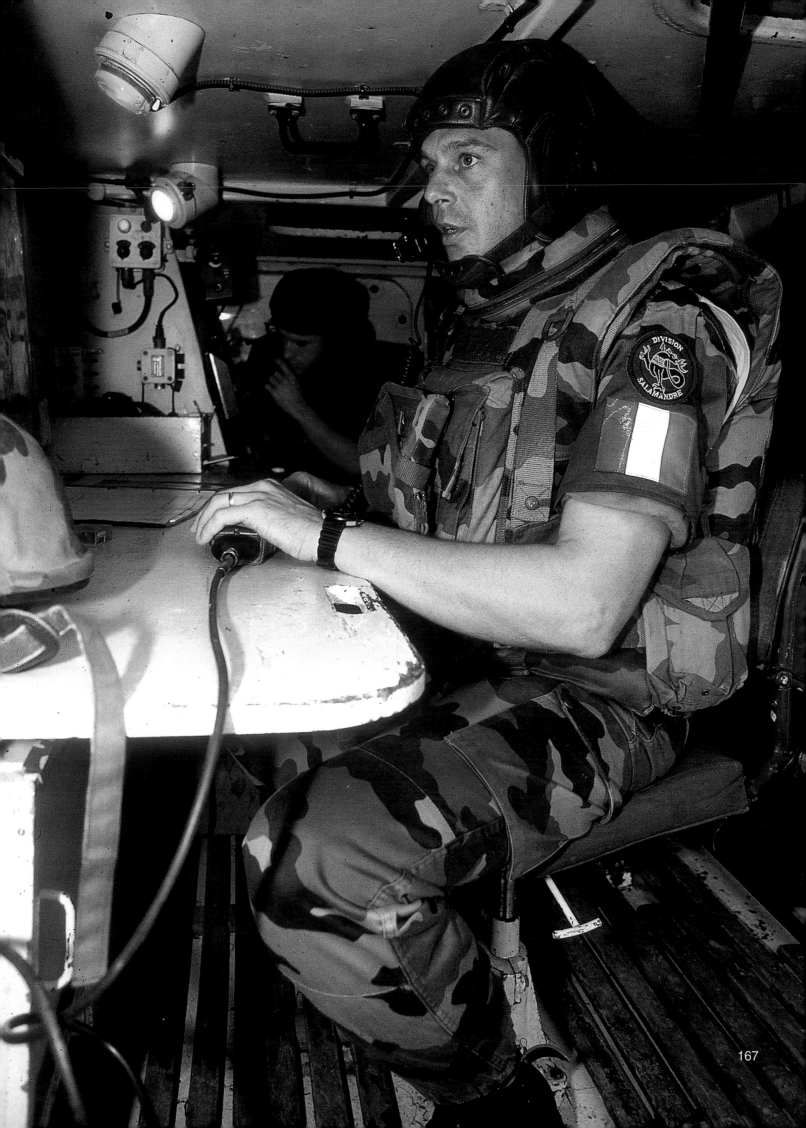

CBI: BASE AND INSTRUCTION COMPANY

In the context of the Army's reorganisation plan 'Armée 2002' each regiment now has a Base and Instruction Company, entrusted with the training of the new recruits.

In the 2e REP, the name remains but remember that in the Foreign Legion, basic training for new legionaries is carried out at the 4e RE at Castelnaudary. The principal objective of the CBI is to support the man in the field and beyond mere parachute training, there are other forms of training which prepare the legionary for operations in their particular environments.

Thus an instruction cell for hand-to-hand fighting and for maintaining law and order were set up to train legionaries who were to be sent to the Balkans. The CBI also manages the TAP training because, and this is unusual in the Army, the Legion paratroopers learn to jump in the REP not in the Army.

One word about the Legionaries' mess run by a young officer and a warrant-officer which gives the legionaries some daily comfort in their time-off, applying the age-old motto, 'Legio Patria Nostra'.

The company also ensures that certain obscure but equally vital tasks are carried out, like washing the company's combat uniforms, and preparing hot meals, and supplying various messes. Essential tasks for bolstering morale.

Rear Base

At the rear, the CBI looks after the thousand and one things which keep the machine running, leaving all the time to the combat companies for operational training. It is the CBI which is responsible for running the regiment's accounts, distributing pay (the old tradition of putting the pay in the soldier's képi has disappeared now that legionaries have bank accounts).

As is the case with the 5th company, the CBI is also a strategic reserve of hardened fighters who can reinforce the combat companies in a tight spot.

Given its position on Corsica, the 2e REP's CBI can also carry out public service missions, like fire-fighting or installing first-aid posts during a natural disaster.

Above:
A Legion paratrooper on guard at the entrance to Raffalli camp, during the daily ceremony of the flag.
(Yves Debay)

Below.
The 'Greens' of the '1re' warm up on the obstacle course. Soon they will receive specialised courses, like maintaining order, given by CBI instructors.
(Yves Debay)

Above: **In the REP as elsewhere, the accounts must be well-kept, just as this CCL adjudant is doing. After thirty years' service in the Foreign Legion, he is responsible for all equipment bookkeeping.**
(Yves Debay)

TAP TRAINNING

As has been mentioned above, the REP is the only airborne regiment in France to train its legionaries in parachute jumping itself. Thanks to the wreck of a Transall which was recovered in the mountains of Corsica after an accident, the regiment now has the means of simulating jump sessions.

Our photographs show a young sergeant of Flemish origin, a born instructor, teaching the rudiments to recently-arrived legionaries.
In a special instruction room, they are also taught how to come down by parachute, what to do in the case of an incident, how to land.

Ground instruction lasts two weeks and as soon as a plane becomes available, the new paratroopers get their wings.

They need six jumps to get the famous 'plaque à vélo' (wings), one at night, one with opening of the reserve parachute, and one when fully equipped.

Left: **Studying how to stand at the door is also studied**
(Yves Debay)

In the Legion The 'Padre' is something of a character. In a little improvised chapel, set up at Raljovac, in Bosnia,
he is contemplating a Virgin with child painted by a legionary from the 2e REP during the worst moments of the Sarajevo Siege.

Above:
Harness work in order to get used to working 'under sail'.
(Yves Debay)

THE LEGIONNAIRES' MESS

Like with every regiment, the 2e REP has its own mess where the legionaries can relax after days which are usually very full. It has a supermarket where the Green Berets can buy all they need, the little things which are not necessarily regulation but which make daily life campaigning a bit cosier; and regimental souvenirs. All at very hard to beat prices.

Left:
Training is not only carried out at the CBI and between two overseas postings, it carries on intensively at Calvi in order to keep up the challenge and to improve. Here a lieutenant in the 4e does not seem too.
(Yves Debay)

THE 'AMICALE DES LEGIONNAIRES PARACHUTISTES'

Tradition and respect for the old Veterans is one of the pillars of the Foreign Legion. The 2e REP does not escape this rule, particularly when the regiment celebrated the 50th anniversary of its creation.

The veterans are the heart of the 'Amicale de Légionnaires Parachutistes'. It is based in Paris and rejoins the regiment on Camerone Day and the St-Michel's day celebrations. Some try another jump, but owing to lack of credits, the tradition is dying off.

The Feast of the Archangel, the patron saint of parachutists is always an opportunity for happy get togethers between old and young Legionaries.

Right:
Here the 'Grands Anciens' (Great Veterans) parade on the occasion of St Michael's Feast day.
(Yves Debay)

TRADITIONS

The Foreign Legion takes a good part of its strength from a fantastic team spirit kept up by numerous traditions and a sharpened sense of camaraderie. In the REP as elsewhere in the Legion, the following big principals are cultivated and kept up: the Will to serve well, a sense of Honour and discipline, love of work well done and a cult of memories.

Full dress uniform is both sober and brilliant and is kept for the important days and symbolises the eternal Legion, with the white képi, the green and red épaulettes, the blue belt, green tie and seniority stripes. Tradition requires that the insignia of the regiments and the companies be triangular.

In combat, the REP can be distinguished by its green beret bearing the insignia of the metropolitan airborne troops.

The legionary's year is full of celebrations. Camerone Day, a very solemn day celebrated by the Legion every 30 April as with St Michel, on 29 September; the Archangel is the patron saint of paratroopers.

A few days after Christmas Day which is celebrated

'en famille' to remind everybody that the Legion is a great family, Epiphany is celebrated upon a chosen theme. This is an opportunity which enables officers and legionaries to fraternise. The 'King' is chosen amongst the older NCOs to counsel the Corps Commander. The Royal Cortege visits all the messes and the streets of Calvi. Often light punishments are cancelled and leave granted. The celebrations often end up in the bars of the town and the king can decide that, for example, the children of the town need not go to school on the day of the feast…

Singing is also important for all the regiments in the Legion. The regiment's song is 'la Légion Marche'. The 'Boudin' is also often sung usually at the beginning of corps' dinners.

These traditions are far from being heavy; they have made the Legion and they do not stop the regiment from being a community of young warriors able to accept any challenge in this modern world.

(Yves Debay)

(Yves Debay)

(Yves Debay)

2e REP SONG

REFRAIN
Nous sommes les hommes des troupes d'assaut,
Soldats de la vieille Légion,
Demain brandissant nos drapeaux,
En vainqueurs nous défilerons,
Nous n'avons pas seulement des armes,
Mais le diable marche avec nous,
Ha, ha, ha, ha, ha, ha, car nos aînés de la Légion,
Se battant là-bas, nous emboîtons le pas.
I
La Légion marche vers le front,
En chantant nous suivons,
Héritiers de ses traditions,
Nous sommes avec elle.
II
Pour ce destin de chevalier,
Honneur, Fidélité,
Nous sommes fiers d'appartenir au 2e REP.

ACKNOWLEDGEMENTS

This book would not have seen the light of day had it not been for the help I received over the last few years from all the Legion parachutists and their officers who had to put up with this civilian and his funny habit of photographing everything and asking a whole lot of questions.

In the Foreign Legion, the men learn to identify themselves through their leader, so today it is to Colonel *Bouquin*, the present Corps Commander of the 2e REP, that I extend my official thanks.

The other commanding officers must not be forgotten and I would like to thank in particular Lieutenant-Colonels *Wabinski*, *Coevoët*, *Gaussères*, *Poulet* — with the memory of a helmet lost at Toulouse-Francazal in 1988 and found again at Sarajevo in 1993 —, *Dary*, *Puga* and *Prévost*.

Many thanks to friend *Guermeu* who got me a jump with the prestigious REP at the time when that sort of thing was still possible.

All the Commandants have a special place in the realisation of this book and in particular Commandant *Zanolini*, my "censor and corrector".

I would also like to thank Capitaines *Fouga* — in memory of being towed in a sledge laden with a certain "hops-based liquid" and getting lost in a snow-storm —, Messager for his kindness and the high quality of his Legion welcome, *Sabjic* in memory of the "Cousins".

Also Capitaines *Desmeules*, *Meunier* and *de Bessombes* of the CEA in memory of his welcome to *Philipovici*, Capitaine *Lobel* at the CEITO, Capitaine *Lardet* of the 1re company on the bridge at Mitrovica and at Calvi as well as Capitaine *Lesquer* "twenty metres under".This message will perhaps reach Capitaine *Perez-Pria* — as a souvenir of a few good bottles of Bordeaux saved from the looters in Brazzaville.

Lieutenants *de la Chapelle* and *Dupont*.

Major *Henri* in the NCO's mess at Sarajevo.

Adjudant-chef *Deptula* of the CCL, bureau EM for the countless coffees drunk in his office.

Adjudants *Thimuran*, *Weiss* and *Gourillon*, remembering a few good nights together.

Adjudants Steele of the Recce unit, *Jacquet* — remembering a good four-thousander over Calvi Bay — , *Smitt* (5e Compagnie) and *El Waadi* remembering Almandin, Brazza and Kosovo.

My thanks also to Sergent-Chefs *Palomba* (the man who whispers in the ears of to dogs), B. Raubenheimer, *Philips* and Sergent *Pelote* all "my opposite numbers" for having turned the archives upside down...

To Sergent *Anglais* of the MILAN unit, Sergent-Chef *Plaiter*, Sergent *Deswaef* and Sergent *Glover*.

A not-so-good memory prevents me from naming all the men in the REP who helped me with this book, but the place they have in my heart and my thoughts is real enough.

So my thanks to you all.

This book was directed by Alexandre THERS

Lay-out by Jean-Marie MONGIN and Antoine POGIOLLI. Insignia photographs by Eric MICHELETTI © *Histoire & Collections*.

© *Histoire & Collections 2002.*

SA au capital de 182 938,82 €

5, avenue de la République
F-75541 Paris Cédex 11 - FRANCE
Telephone: (33-1) 40 21 18 20
Fax: (33-1) 47 00 51 11

This book has been designed, typed, laid out and processed by *Histoire & Collections* and the *Studio Graphique Armes & Collections* , fully on integrated computer equipment

Printed by
KSG-Elkar/KSG-Danona
in october 2002 European Union